# Candid comments from readers of this new book

*"I have been around combat in the Marine Corps, and with cops for most of my life. This is the first serious change in how we must look at SURVIVAL combat. It is not so much technique as it is a mental frame of mind. It has been most refreshing to read."*

P. Neskow, Barrington, IL

*"It was the best book I have ever read on Self Protection. It gives a 360 degree understanding of the subject. I possessed the physical side and understanding but I could never fully understand the mental part. Once I finished your book I realized I could get the job done if need be... without hesitation. The way you communicate so clearly on the subject, I can see you have survived violent encounters. A lot of people who teach Self Protection never have -- its just theory."*

Shane Parisi, Mountain View, CA

*"The TFT material has shed light on the grey area of violence. So simple to understand, anyone can pick it up and learn the truth about surviving an undesirable situation. One of the most significant reads I've come across. I highly recommend it!"*

Justin Negrete, Madison, WI

*"Having survived a tour in Nam as a combat medic I can attest to the mental fortitude necessary to counter a violent battle. Only wish this book was written 40 years ago!"*

Dennis Aurilia, Parkland, FL

*"I always thought I had a good combat mindset, use of color codes in my everyday life, and an understanding of what I would do if confronted with a life and death situation. I had half a picture! This is a whole different world! The simplest and best explanation I have ever heard of why when violence is the answer it truly is the only answer."*

Todd W. Carr, Marion, NY

# HOW TO

# SURVIVE

## THE MOST CRITICAL
## 5 SECONDS OF YOUR LIFE

TIM LARKIN
&
CHRIS RANCK-BUHR

Third Edition

Printed in the United States of America.

How to Survive the Most Critical 5 Seconds of Your Life
by Tim Larkin & Chris Ranck-Buhr

First Edition: 2008
Second Edition 2009

ISBN 978-1-61539-310-7

The TFT Group
Straitview Publishing
325 E Washington St, #207
Sequim, WA 98382

*Dedicated to everyone who*
*made it back home alive . . .*

*and to the memory of*
*those who didn't.*

# Foreword

*"The art of war is simple enough. Find out where the enemy is. Get at him as soon as you can. Strike him as hard as you can and as often as you can, and keep moving on."* — *General U.S. Grant*

There are many different reasons you might start reading this book, but the only reason to finish it is if you want to protect yourself and your family from violence. That's it. You see, I'm not just going to give you a few techniques to ward off a local thug. I don't want to level the playing field. I want to skew it in your favor. In other words, I want to make sure that if you're ever in a violent situation, you walk away with your life.

But to do that, you need to know something about the principles of what you're doing. It's educating yourself about the facts of violence. Without it, you're doing what everyone else is doing— just learning techniques for specific situations. And by the time you finish this book, you'll understand why that's a recipe for disaster.

It truly amazes me how many people just stumble into various martial arts or combat sports never having once considered why they're doing it. If you're training your body to participate in competitions, then you'll find numerous martial arts and combat sports that provide excellent instruction and challenging forms of competition. These give you the opportunity to exercise your abilities in a safe situation, with rules and supervision agreed upon in advance.

Combat sports can teach you effective tactics for fighting, and they're great for getting into shape. Unfortunately, however, if "sport fighting" is your thing, this book will not say a thing to you. I'm talking about real violence, the kind we all want to avoid. I'm talking about learning to effectively deal with real life-or-death threats. And that's completely different from combat sport fighting.

At this point, you might be wondering why you can't do both. Or maybe you're wondering why you should know how to fight at all. Maybe you're thinking that's why we have social institutions such as the police—to defend us and keep us safe from life-or-death situations.

But this book addresses the place where social communication ends and real violence begins—places where you have no control over your opponent. In other words, this book addresses those situations we all try to pretend don't exist.

The real question is, if you're unfortunate enough to find yourself in a life-or-death situation, will you have the ability to defend yourself and your family? Because in that moment, nothing else will matter.

If you want to know the truth about self-defense, read on. You might not like what I have to say. But if you keep reading, I guarantee you'll come to see the truth: There's only one way you'll ever be prepared to walk away from a life-or-death situation.

—*Tim Larkin*

# PART ONE:

# VIOLENCE IN YOUR LIFE TODAY

# Chapter One:

## The Unthinkable Happens

*"Any man who is a man may not, in honor, submit to threats of violence. But many men who are not cowards are simply unprepared for acts of human savagery. They have not thought about it (incredible as this may appear to anyone who reads the papers or listens to the news) and they just don't know what to do. When they look right into the face of depravity and violence they are astonished and confounded."*
—Jeff Cooper

It doesn't make you a coward to acknowledge that you have no idea what to do in a life-or-death violent situation. In fact, it means that you have the courage to accept that there are people out there who will act in unpredictable and irrational ways to get what they want—a fact many people blithely ignore. And if you're reading this book, it means you've taken that acceptance a step further, and you're ready to do something about it.

Since I started Target-Focus Training (TFT), I've traveled extensively, giving seminars on how to use violence as a tool for survival. One of my most significant trips occurred when I toured Asia. I had the good fortune to travel to Singapore, Jakarta, Manila, Shanghai, and Hong Kong, and every step of the journey, the specter of violence loomed in the background. Most of my hotels had a barricade, all my cars were searched for bombs, and each guest was searched every time they reentered the hotel. My hosts represented some of the most influential people in each of these regions, and they all welcomed my message: violence is the only way to combat violence.

Why?

Because the people living in these cities live every day with the threat of violence entering their lives in a real and dramatic fashion. And they don't just face the threat of criminal violence. Political violence, terrorists, kidnappers, business rivals—all use violence as a means to solve problems.

These are clients who take a plan for asocial violence seriously. It's not that they're violent people themselves or ever want to use the knowledge. But when you've seen political assassinations over a mayoral election, when you've seen a political opponent's entire family slaughtered, you realize there are those who are very comfortable solving any conflict with violence—and you realize that you'd better be ready if they ever come gunning for you.

It quickly becomes clear that if you are unfortunate enough to get involved with people like this, you may very well find yourself in a situation where using violence is your only answer. I share this because rarely have I found my message so well received—ironically in a part of the world that was the birthplace of martial arts.

### Why Can't We All Just Get Along?

There are two types of people who won't find much to help them in this book: those who think violence is never justifiable, and those who think violence is the answer to everything. One thing that will become very clear over the course of this book is that violence is an extremely negative thing. I don't recommend it as a solution to any but the most desperate of conflicts. In other words, violence is what you use when every other choice has been taken from you. So why can't we all just get along?

A perfect example occurs in the war against terror. Whether you back the war or not, our soldiers face a committed enemy who is willing to do whatever it takes to further its cause. They don't think twice about beheading civilians or sacrificing innocent lives—including their own—to make a point. Their commitment to their

3

cause is total and even the wounded will booby-trap themselves just to kill a couple more soldiers 'for the cause.' Against such an enemy you cannot afford to respond with a litigious, law enforcement mentality.

We cannot win by trying to 'arrest' the enemy. The cold, hard fact is that we must kill the enemy in large enough numbers to break the back of the insurgents. It is politically incorrect to point such facts out, but that, quite frankly, is the nature of war. You don't have to like war, but you have to accept it for what it is. A soldier overseas may not like what he has to do, but if he wants to survive—and if he wants his friends and family to remain safe—he has no choice but to respond to the enemy in kind.

But this mentality is not just dangerous to soldiers on the battlefields of the Middle East. The same applies to you. You cannot afford such a litigious mentality when faced with real, asocial violence. You must respond by injuring the other guy as fast as you can. You can't rely on running or blocking anymore than the military can use law enforcement guidelines to defeat a 'kill or be killed' enemy.

I don't advocate responding to antisocial behavior with violence; nor do I believe violence will solve our social or political problems. But whether it's a soldier facing a committed, fanatical enemy or a businessman facing an asocial recidivist criminal, the only response that will get the job done is to use the tool of violence. That's why you must ask yourself right now, "Do I really know how to use the tool of violence?" You simply can't wait to ask it until asocial violence is imminent. By then the stakes are far too high.

# Chapter Two:

## Surviving the Most Critical Five Seconds of Your Life

*"What can be successfully willed must first be seen and understood." —Brigadier General S.L.A. Marshall*

There's nothing artistic about violence; it's an instinctive survival tool, like swimming. Once you've learned the basics, you're set for life. You don't walk around every day wondering what you'd do if you fell into a swimming pool: "Let's see, first I'd tread water, then I'd follow that up with a couple of neat butterfly strokes..." You just know that if you fall in, you'll swim to the edge and get out of the water.

An Olympic swimmer who trains every day will always be able to swim faster, further, and with more grace than the average person who learned as a kid and only ever gets wet in the shower. But under normal conditions, neither of them will drown. Whether you're an Olympic swimmer or an amateur, if you fall into a life-or-death situation in the water, you swim to avoid death. Violence is the same: a simple, utilitarian life skill. And as in swimming, the only arbiter of success is survival. If you make it out alive, you did the right thing.

Serious violent conflict rarely lasts more than five seconds. It doesn't take much to put even the biggest man down, and five seconds is more than enough time to cause serious injury. On the other hand, that means you don't have the luxury of time to think or take up a fancy kung-fu stance. You get time only to act, cause an effect, and continue to act.

So why is violence so important to survival? Because violence works on everyone. Superior physical ability, knowledge, experience, and iron will are all trumped by the thumb in the eye. There is nothing anyone can do to make themselves immune to the laws of the physical universe.

Bullets are not swayed by opinion or presence; they are maddeningly impartial. In other words, everyone can do violence, and no one is immune.

## Surviving is not Enough

Some people will argue that it's not necessary to become familiar with the tool of violence—that it's enough to know self-defense and be prepared for different situations. Well, I'm here to tell you that those tools might give you the ability to survive a violent situation. But is survival enough? Consider these examples:

At the age of 32, Jim, a man with years of martial arts training, was attacked by a meth-crazed mugger in an unprovoked homicidal assault. He was stabbed three times. He's still with us because his girlfriend attempted to stop the mugger. She was stabbed twice in the neck and bled-out before the paramedics could arrive.

John is a police officer with 12 years on the force and numerous defensive tactics courses under his belt. On a bright August day he pulled over a '79 Chevy Camaro for a dangerous lane change while speeding. As he approached, the 6'5", 262 lb very drunk driver got out to contest John's decision to stop him.

Before John finished the verbal warning he'd used a 1,000 times before, the driver bum-rushed him, lifted him off the deck, and slammed him to the pavement. Following the techniques he'd been drilled in, John fumbled for his pepper spray while the driver laughed and repeatedly pounded John's head against the pavement.

John lost consciousness as kicks to the head and torso rained down from the alcohol-fueled rage. He's still on the force today but in an admin job. Nerve damage to his right side is pretty severe.

His facial reconstructive surgery went well and surgeons think he'll regain 90% control of his facial muscles, eventually.

John's defensive tactics training was extensive. The board that reviewed the video of the incident stated John responded exactly as he was trained.

Jamie is a survivor, too.

She did everything the serial rapist asked. But the self-defense course she took never gave her a technique for the way this 234 lb brute held her on the floor of her apartment. When she said she'd do whatever he wanted, he responded by punching her face and breaking her jaw. From there it got worse.

After 3 reconstructive surgeries, she eventually recovered from the beating, but not from the trauma of rape.

Her self-defense training had great techniques and real life scenarios. Hell, it even had an instructor in a padded suit attacking them, one she could hit as hard as she wanted.

And yet she still fell victim to this violent attack.

All of these people are survivors. They lived after a vicious, unprovoked encounter with real violence. But are their lives what they were before the attacks? What they've suffered should be enough to convince you: survival is not enough.

**What Went Wrong?**

So what was lacking in the training of these three survivors?

I've asked this question many times before, and I always hear two responses: mind-set and will. Mind-set is by far was the most popular response. Most who respond with this answer feel the survivors' training failed to develop the proper mind-set to survive and win these encounters.

Those that offer "will" as the lacking ingredient usually state that the training of the three survivors failed to provide them the "will" to use violence.

Makes sense, right? There's only one problem: no one knows what it really means. They're buzzwords, and when you're faced with real violence, they're worse than useless.

All the talk about 'mind-set' in this industry makes everyone sound the same. Most people still believe you need to be in a certain 'state' to be able to respond to violence. Color charts are drafted and everyone feels good about how to get ready to 'kick some ass.'

And then there's 'will.'

Some people stated that the three survivors lacked the will to do injury and this was a failure of their training. But how do you train will? Think about how useful will is when it comes to things like losing weight or working out. Besides, when you consider the situation, all three of these survivors were in desperate situations. In the midst of these horrible, vicious attacks, they almost certainly had the will to survive.

A lot of people will lecture you on mind-set and come up with numerous drills to 'instill the will to kill.' But neither mind-set nor will is what lacked in any of the survivors' training. In fact, large amounts of the training in all three of the survivors' cases focused on developing proper mind-set and will. But neither was there when they needed it.

That is because mind-set and will are not training objectives. Proper training develops everything needed to survive and win. The problem is there is very little proper training offered to the general public.

The point here isn't to belittle these three survivors. They did everything right according to how they'd been trained. The problem, then, isn't with the survivors: it's with their training.

## Making the Critical Choices

At this point, it's time for you to make a decision. Do you want to survive a violent encounter, or do you want to win? Because in the moment when someone comes at you, you won't have time to consider mind-set, will, or any of the other things self-defense instructors commonly go on about. You'll only have time to act.

If you're still with me, you're probably starting to realize that proper training is the key to becoming comfortable with violence. When I say comfortable, I don't mean that you should look forward to or seek to engage in violent encounters. What I mean is, you need to be comfortable using violence in a violent situation the same way you're comfortable swimming in a drowning situation: as a tool to survive.

## The Most Common Mistakes People Make When Picking a Self-Defense System

So now that you're ready to learn how to defend yourself—how to win a violent encounter, not just survive it—how do you decide what to do? How can you avoid a program that trains you in the same mistakes the three survivors above learned to make?

When it comes to self-defense systems, there are a lot of choices out there. You've got everything from karate at the local Y to aggressive combat sports to 'hardcore' hand-to-hand combat types on the Internet. With all these choices, how is someone supposed to know what really works and what doesn't? Here are the most common mistakes most people make when confronted with choosing a self-defense system:

### 1. Picking a system that takes years to be usable.

If a system won't work for you until you're a Black Belt, it's not going to do you any good next week, let alone tomorrow. If it's going to take you a couple of years to learn, then you'd better pray you don't run into trouble until then. And let's be honest: that time frame is just not realistic. In a world that's dangerous right now, you need something that's useful to you right now, not five years down the road.

### 2. *Picking a system that requires constant practice.*

You never forget how to ride a bike or swim; no matter how long you go without doing it. If you're going to bet your life on a self-defense system, it better work the same way. It does you no good to learn something that requires constant upkeep. Sure, it'll work great as long as you're still training, but what about after you stop? What if it's been a couple of years since you hit the mats? You'll be more than rusty: you could wind up dead! If knowing how to swim means you know how to save yourself from drowning for the rest of your life, doesn't it make sense that a self-defense system should work the same way?

You might think: "But I'm not going to stop training!" Well, that's fine for right now. But you have to plan for all eventualities in the future.

### 3. *Picking a system based on 'cool' techniques.*

The instructor puts on an impressive, spellbinding demo. He's flying all over the place, doing all sorts of amazing and complicated things—heck, he even broke a block of ice with his head! Naturally, you want what he has: that ability, that catlike grace, that power. The only question you have to ask is, when was the last time you saw a serial killer do anything fancy? Or what about in a prison riot? Nothing fancy there—just brutal simplicity. When trying to figure out what to do in a violent situation, look to the people who have the most experience with it: the common criminal element. They know you don't need empty techniques that look 'cool' to get the job done. In violence it's never about how it looks: it's what it does that makes the difference. Make sure your chosen system can tell the two apart and show you how to get the job done, no matter what you look like doing it.

### 4. *Picking a system based on competition.*

Physical competition in and of itself is a wonderful thing. There's nothing quite like pitting yourself against another person to see who's faster, stronger, or more cunning. There's no high like besting others while basking in the camaraderie that skilled competition brings.

But when your life is on the line, you can't afford to compete: the stakes are just too high. Violence is, by definition, unfair. If all of your training is for fair competition, you've put yourself at an unfair disadvantage on the street. I can guarantee that the criminal who has decided to stab you in the neck isn't going to play by the rules.

### 5. *Picking a system that doesn't take into account all body types.*

Be honest: are you in the best shape of your life? Even if you are, all it takes is a couple of years behind a desk, and a couple of kids, to end up like the rest of us. If you're training somewhere where the instructor, all his senior students, and the best of the rest in the class look like a gang of clones, you can bet that the system favors that body type. Whether it's tall and lean with long legs at a Karate dojo or shorter and solidly stout in a Judo club, you're only going to do well there if you look just like them. If you don't, well, it's not going to work so well for you. Your best bet is training that fits any body type, no matter how tall, short, small or heavy. If you see people of all shapes and sizes practicing, you can bet it'll work for you.

### 6. *Picking a system based on a hit movie.*

You'd be amazed how often this happens! Sure, we'd all like to fight like Spiderman ... and while we're at it, why don't we fly like Superman, too? Movies are, by definition, fake. Anything you see in a movie is choreographed and computer-generated. It's all a set-up: they had to do 800 takes and edit the crap out of it to get the final result that wowed you in the theater. In real life violence, you only get one take, and there's no movie magic to save the day. Keep the fantasy in the theater and off the mats.

### 7. *Picking a system that only works when everyone agrees to play by certain rules.*

This can mean anything from competition (where the contestants are bound by rules) to training in prearranged patterns that never change. The problem with this kind of training is that in violence, anything goes. Set patterns get shattered and that one scenario you trained and trained for will go down in the most unexpected way possible, taking you completely by surprise. Make sure any system you choose takes into account the chaos that exists naturally in violent conflict.

### 8. *Picking a system that doesn't look like the violence you see on the news.*

If it doesn't look like the violence you see on the news, it's not going to work off the mats or outside the dojo. Period.

### 9. *Picking a system that doesn't account for multiple attackers.*

The biggest fallacy out there is that violent assault is going to go down just like an episode of heroic single combat: you vs. him. Statistics show it's much more likely to be you, him, and all his friends. Make sure any system you choose can show you how to deal with everyone who's going to be there.

### 10. *Picking a system that doesn't account for common, modern weaponry (knives, sticks, guns).*

This is the killer. Nothing is more surprising than bringing a 'spinning backhand' to a gunfight. Or expecting a stand-up boxing match only to get knifed in the process. Every system can show you how to deal with a single unarmed guy. Fewer systems can show you how to deal with a stick or knife. Only a couple even bother to bring up the gun. You need to make sure you find the one that handles all of these things at once, no matter how many people you're dealing with or what they're packing.

# Chapter Three

## Inside the Criminal Mind

*"Although we must change the ways we protect our country, we must also guard against policies that appear attractive but offer little real protection and may even impede our ability to protect ourselves." —Richard Burr*

So now you know how not to train for self-defense. Unfortunately, the best way to train for self-defense is to look to the people who are going to be perpetrating the violence: the criminals themselves. The idea of fighting like a criminal might not sound very appealing, but believe me, when you're face to face with someone who's ready and willing to kill you, you want to have all the advantages you can get.

Your biggest problem is that you want to go in playing by the rules. But don't worry—it's not your fault. You're sane. You're civilized. Your humanity is intact. You've got empathy, and heck, the rules are really, really nice. They've done a lot for us—humans couldn't have walked on the Moon without the rules to help us all work together.

The predators in our society look at life a little ... differently. Sociopathy is a broad term that covers everything from people with personality disorders to psychotics. That doesn't really matter to you, though: what matters is that this person's brain isn't working the same way as the normal, civilized people you meet at work, next door, or at the supermarket.

The main characteristic of a sociopath? A complete lack of awareness about morality and social behavior. That means that a criminal not only won't abide by rules of fair play, there's a good chance he won't even give them a passing thought. You have to understand that this guy will not be worried about pulling dirty tricks, playing fair, or shoving a knife through your eye. He has one thing in mind, and the ends justify the means—even if the "ends" are nothing more than the ten bucks in your wallet or soothing his savage pride.

Until you can approach violence the same way, he will always have an edge. You do understand about morality and fair play. But in the moment your life is in danger, you have to shut that awareness off and go after him—any way possible.

### Isn't It Dangerous to Put This Information Out There?

One of the most common objections I hear from people is, "What if criminals get a hold of this information? Isn't it dangerous to give them access to the kind of information they need to kill and maim other people?"

Well, this would be an excellent objection except for one thing: They already know how to use violence to get what they want!

Do they have all the principles and methods included in this book? No. But they have no problem using violence to get what they want and they know the critical factor that makes violence work: intent!

As I've stated numerous times in my newsletter and DVD products—to be successful with violence you need zero training but you must have intent. If you have years of 'training' and no intent, you lose every time.

Criminals don't waste time learning to use the tool better—they rely on intent alone.

Information I've released has created a fundamental change in the way good people go about truly protecting themselves. At first, for some, the information is uncomfortable, even shocking. But it rings true. My job is not to worry that the criminals will get a hold of this info, but to worry that good people won't. They are the ones who truly need this program. All a criminal would do is look at it and nod his head in agreement.

## An Inside Perspective

This is a perspective on the criminal mind offered to me by a criminal defense attorney:

*"I am an attorney, my job is communication. I represent criminals. They do not communicate in the same way as we do. They do not communicate from the same set of social beliefs.*

*A person under stress, such as a knife to the neck, may not communicate well with adrenaline pounding through the system and blood retreating from the frontal lobes of the brain (where 10,000 years of human civilization lives) to the central brain (where fight, flight or freeze lives).*

*People blurt out the most inappropriate things. Recently a journalist was being kidnapped in Iraq, she wanted to say that she was a journalist; instead she blurted out, 'I'm a vegetarian.'*

*The fact that she thought either phrase would help indicates that she did not understand the concept of the operation. A detachment of Marines solved the problem. If all one has is communications skills, then one must work those words for all they are worth. My first choice remains the equivalent of a detachment of Marines."*     *- Kevin Jamison*

The key here is that the criminal is not operating from the same set of social beliefs you are. You are a well-adjusted, socialized person. Deep down, you believe that there's a way to resolve your problems without anyone getting hurt.

A criminal doesn't.

As social, sane people, we tend to think of violence in social terms—either by framing everything as the school yard David and Goliath or by believing that if we take our social rules with us into the void place we can somehow hang onto our humanity and therefore not stoop to the criminal level.

We tend to think of violence as a force continuum where if he yells at you, you can yell at him. If he pushes you, then you can push him. If he throws a punch, then you can hit back. We also believe that the worst kind of violence, that which results in death, happens somewhere out at the end of this progression, if it gets pushed far enough.

The problem is that it is not necessary to get 'worked up' or walk through all these various steps to get to serious crippling injury or death; punching someone in the throat or stabbing them in the neck is readily available at all times, in all places.

This is what the criminal sociopath knows.

Can someone ramp up through all the steps and whip themselves into a frothy frenzy that ends in killing? Yes. But what the criminal sociopath knows is that he can get there instantaneously. He can go from smiling and shrugging to stabbing in the amount of time it takes him to reach into his pocket. And the really scary part is so can you.

Violence is always available; you just have to choose to do it. You don't need to walk through the social dance one step at a time to get there. You don't need to get ready, or drop into a fighting stance, or give a verbal warning. You can swing the tool of violence whenever you wish, at a moment's notice. And this is exactly what you must to do in the face of asocial violence in order to survive.

## Why are the Thugs Still Winning?

The reason thugs are still using violence, and still winning, certainly isn't that they're smarter. It isn't even that they're stronger—many people who get beaten up and robbed on the streets every day are fitter and stronger than their drug-addicted assailants. The reason muggers win is that they have power. They know what they want, and they know that if they use every violent means at their disposal, they'll get it. They know that:

- If they pull out a knife, you're going to get scared.
- If they put a gun to your head, you're going to freeze.
- If they threaten to kill you, you'll give them anything they demand.

They understand how to use violence in order to cause the effect they want to achieve.

Am I advocating that same approach? No. Learning how to use violence doesn't turn you into a criminal; it changes the balance of power. When you are proficient in the use of this simple system, instead of a threat from a violent stranger causing you to suffer pain, loss or even death, you will be able to cause serious injury to the man, resulting in his complete incapacitation.

You'll understand that if you injure a man in a certain way, you can precisely predict the result. Instead of doubt preventing you from taking action, you'll have the confidence to make the split-second decisions you need to stay alive during the most stressful seconds of your life. When you've undergone this sort of training, you'll have the power—the power to protect yourself and those you love.

## Taking Off The Gloves

In violent conflict there are no rules. No part of the body is out of bounds and there are no gloves to soften the blows. Violence isn't like the choreographed dance moves you see on TV shows and movies. Each side doesn't take turns to swing and parry. One side strikes and the other side gets injured. And usually, the side that causes the first serious injury wins.

When you know how to use violence as a survival tool, you'll be the one doing the striking, the one causing the injuries.

Criminals are not in it for competition. They are committed to a radically different idea: injuring people. In the society we live in, the focus for the law-abiding citizen has been on learning how to keep violence from happening to us—how to deal with a violent attack, how to keep a serial rapist at bay, how to keep the minimum safe distance, how to break the hold and run away.

The myriad techniques available all claim to work, yet never cause debilitating trauma. It's easy to see why you'd want to know hundreds of different ways to keep someone from hurting you. Yet each and every technique you learn has you struggling to survive, without the surety of success the criminal enjoys. The criminal doesn't succeed because he knows how to deal with violence. He succeeds because his specialty is dealing out violence.

# Chapter Four

## Antisocial vs. Asocial Violence

*"Though defensive violence will always be 'a sad necessity' in the eyes of men of principle, it would be still more unfortunate if wrongdoers should dominate just men."* — Saint Augustine

If you listen to people recount their experiences with violence, you'll quickly find that they fall into two distinct groups: those who have survived a true life-or-death confrontation and those who participated in violence as a kind of sport or game.

The first group rarely speaks about the subject. When they choose to share the experience, you'll notice that they are usually brutally honest, and almost always emphasize the fear of the situation. They make it clear that they were forced into action because they had no acceptable alternative. There is no gloating over their surviving the experience, and though many acted heroically, they don't see it that way. They see themselves as fortunate to have survived and they hope never to be in that situation ever again.

Participants in social aggression, however, often revel in retelling the exploit where "they kicked his ass." You'll find yourself sitting through a play-by-play and listening to trash-talk about the other party. These people also give the impression they are ready to participate again should they ever be called upon to defend their honor, a parking space, or a spilled drink after happy hour.

Why the different responses? The first group came in contact with that ultimate specter: unavoidable life-or-death violence. No choice, no retreat, simply fight or die. In other words, the situation wasn't fun. They dealt with it and moved on.

The second group chose violence. They took a situation that was not life threatening and chose to respond with violence. This group enjoyed using violence to gain dominance. It produced a base human reaction of control over another in the pecking order.

Now, that doesn't mean the other guy wasn't "asking for it," so to speak, or that the situation couldn't have escalated to a life-or-death situation. But in this case, using violence as a response was a deliberate choice.

People choose to use violence when they let their egos rule the situation. That's why a victory is enjoyable—it's an ego boost. The unavoidable use of violence produces a very different outcome: the desire to not participate in it ever again.

Raw violence is not something I wish on anyone, but I teach its use and methodology because when you need it you can't have enough knowledge of the subject. And quite frankly, the more competent I make you in that subject, the less likely you are to waste your time choosing to use violence in a social situation.

## Antisocial Violence

The violence that comes from social posturing is avoidable; it is often loud, dramatic, and instantly recognizable. You get to see it coming. And that means you can dodge it if you choose to.

If you don't choose to (or cannot) leave, these sorts of problems can be handled with the social tools we're all familiar with. We've all talked our way out of a bad situation—you wouldn't have made it this far in life if you weren't good at negotiating. We all know how to calm someone down. We all know how to capitulate. We also all know how to act like a jerk and add fuel to the fire and turn an argument into a shouting match, a shouting match into a fist fight. The important point here is that in social situations, you have a choice.

Antisocial violence is also eminently survivable. The typical goal in a bar fight is not to kill anyone—it's simply to best the other person and dominate them physically. Does this mean you can't be killed in a bar fight? Of course not. What I'm saying is that the death rate in the typical Saturday night punch-up is far lower than one would expect—and most fatalities are accidental. You can get killed in a bar fight, or an argument over a parking space, or any other trivial social status confrontation. It's just highly unlikely.

## Asocial Violence

Asocial violence, on the other hand, cannot be handled with social tools and is far less survivable. Negotiating with a serial killer is like arguing with a bullet: if it's coming your way, words are not going to deflect it. If someone has decided to stab you to death, capitulation only makes their work easier.

## Confusing the Two

So how do you know whether you're dealing with antisocial or asocial violence? Once you understand the difference between the two, it's really as easy as telling a peacock from a tiger. One involves posturing and ego, the other is all about survival. The big problem arises when we confuse the two—when we don't know there's a difference between competition and destruction, between antisocial and asocial violence.

Think about a bar fight. It looks and sounds like it does because it is a display, meant to be seen and heard by all those in attendance. The participants have no intentions of seriously injuring each other; in fact, if you interrupted them and offered them handguns to shoot at each other, they'd probably think you were insane.

Asocial violence is brutally streamlined by comparison. It starts quietly, suddenly, and unmistakably. It's knocking a man down and kicking him to death. It's one person beating another with a tire iron until he stops moving. It's stabbing someone 14 times. It's pulling the gun and firing round after round into him until he goes down and then stepping in close to make sure the last two go through the brain.

If you're a sane, socialized person, those images make you physically ill. That's because you recognize them for what they are: asocial violence. The breakdown of everything we humans hold dear, the absence of our favorite construct, the very fabric of society itself. It's an awful place where there's no such thing as a 'fair fight' or honor. It's the place where there are no rules and anything goes. It's the place where people kill and get killed.

## The Essential Differences Between Antisocial and Asocial Violence

There's a short and easy way to sum this up:

### Antisocial Violence:

- Is avoidable
- Is survivable
- Can be solved using social skills

### Asocial Violence:

- Is lethal
- Is unaffected by social skills
- Requires decisive action.

## Antisocial and Asocial Acts

Once people understand these critical differences, they rarely confuse antisocial and asocial violence. There's still the risk, though, that they may confuse antisocial and asocial actions. Antisocial actions are threatening and potentially dangerous, but there's still the possibility of dealing with them through basic social skills.

Asocial actions, on the other hand, are kill or be killed.

Essentially, the difference revolves around the idea of communication. Antisocial behavior is in the realm of communication (albeit the bad end of communication). This means that though the other guy is threatening you (for example, holding a knife to neck and demanding your valuables), he is still attempting, in the crudest way possible, to communicate with you. Holding a knife to your throat and saying, "Give me your money" is still in the realm of communication. If it was a truly asocial act, he wouldn't bother telling you what he wanted. He would simply take it.

If you use your social skills towards antisocial behavior you may be able to diffuse the situation and essentially 'make the bad man go away' by giving him what he wants and then hoping he chooses to honor this questionable contract and leave. I'm sure you notice the qualifiers in there, and that's because there's an inherent risk in trying to reason with someone in this situation. There is still a possibility of resolving this situation without violence. If this is how it goes down, then we would say this was a successful use of your social skills to handle antisocial behavior.

However, if at any time the situation devolves to physical violence, it ceases to be in the realm of antisocial and is in the realm of asocial violence. In this realm, there is no communication—only action. The goal is not to continue dialogue but to end the interaction.

The only way to gain control of this situation is for you to be the one successfully using the tool of violence. The only way to be guaranteed success with this tool is to cause an objective injury on the other guy and continue to do so until he is nonfunctional.

There are no gray areas in antisocial vs. asocial. If you have a choice whether to respond with violence, then that situation is in the realm of social/antisocial. When you have no choice then it is asocial. In other words, if it's fight or die, you're dealing with asocial violence.

# Chapter Five

## When To Engage

*"The world is filled with violence. Because criminals carry guns, we decent law-abiding citizens should also have guns. Otherwise they will win and the decent people will lose."*
—James Earl Jones

The reason I spend so much time on the difference between social and asocial violence is because it's absolutely essential to know what kind you're dealing with. Some people think just because I train the use of violence as the ultimate survival tool that it means I advocate responding to any situation with violence. Nothing could be further from the truth.

Here's a classic example of a trained reaction to avoidable violence. Matt, one of my Mastery students posted this sad story on our TFT Mastery Forum:

"In Dallas we have a famous little nightspot called the Gypsy Tea Room. You can see acts like Ben Harper, Edie Brickel, Old 97's, etc. "

"Recently, a father of two teenage girls decided to take his girls to an end-of-summer show before they left for college. Before the show was over he ended up having a severed spinal cord injury and can feel nothing from the neck down. Why?"

"Needless social violence."

"He engaged a 'skinhead' in a verbal altercation because the skinhead made a comment to one of his daughters. This led to male posturing, yelling, etc. And then the skinhead opened his 'toolbox of violence' first and pummeled the guy to the floor."

"As the father was on the floor the skinhead stomped down on his face and severed the man's spinal cord somewhere between C1-C5. This all occurred right in front of his two daughters."

"Situations like this remind me of the many reasons I thank God TFT came into my life."

"Why?"

"Most people would think that I would say this because if I were this father I would have kicked the skinhead's ass because of my training."

"WRONG!"

"Because of what I learned from TFT I would not have engaged the skinhead in any verbal altercation. If the skinhead tried to start a verbal altercation I would have gotten my girls and myself out of the club immediately. All the while trying to look like a coward—the wimp."

"Don't get me wrong; if the situation were going to become violent I would have made it very violent. But, more than likely, simply leaving the club would have saved this man a lifetime of paralysis and spared his daughters from witnessing this horrific act."

"TFT gives us a plan, choices, and many tools to pull out of the toolbox. As cliché as it may sound, life is about the choices we make. Thank you, TFT, for the education that you've given myself and countless others in order that we may make the right choices when it come to violence."

"The father is a local high-end trim carpenter and has a home in a very wealthy part of Dallas. The club that he was hurt in, along with the band, had a fund-raising 5k run for him this weekend. The skinhead fled to California and was arrested later that week."

"I firmly believe that the skinhead's stomp to the face was merely intended to cause cosmetic damage not severe the man's spinal cord."

"The skinhead knew how to use violence as a tool but clearly did not understand targets and injury to those targets."

"I am constantly amazed that we get the question 'does this stuff work?' from many of the students. This 'stuff' works far better than they understand. Violence is at work everyday, everywhere."

This story, in all its horror, graphically illustrates a key point. When violence is the answer, it's the only answer. At that point, if you don't know how to use it then you're screwed—and very likely dead!

But since it rarely is the answer, if you don't know when to use it, then you're equally screwed (and may wish you were dead)!

"So then I took my thumb and I dug his eyeball right out of his skull."

Some of you might be cringing at the above statement. Some of you might think it's unnecessary exaggeration, or something you didn't want to hear.

But that statement is exactly, word-for-word, what a Master Instructor stunned participants with at a recent live training in San Diego after he'd repeatedly gotten the question, "... how do I know when I should use what you're teaching?"

See, if you want to know whether the situation warrants extreme violence, take the situation you're suggesting and add that phrase to the end of it.

Try it out with these two examples:

1. *"The drunk just flipped me off and told me to #$%@ myself, so then I took my thumb and I dug his eyeball right out of his skull."*

2. *"As I turned, the gangbanger stabbed me, cutting me in the ribs, so then I took my thumb and I dug his eyeball right out of his skull."*

Put that way, it's pretty obvious which situation warrants the response. If you can't finish your "self defense" question with that phrase then it's not a situation violence can help with. Period.

Why? Because I teach how to do one thing and one thing only: how to completely shut off another human being. It's what I mean when I say "using violence as a survival tool." It's a limited tool, for sure, but one that's necessary (and priceless) if your life is on the line.

## When To Act

It's a romantic notion—using a combat sport or martial art to 'better' a bad guy—and one that's far more seductive to think about than gouging the eye out of the socket of some guy who comes at you with a knife. But you have to leave the romance on the movie theater floor and deal with the reality of violence as it's practiced in everyday life.

Hopefully, you'll never have to use the kind of violence I'm talking about. But if you're ever in doubt about whether you should use it or not, remember the advice from above.

Using violence to solve social problems is like using dynamite to open your car door. It'll do the job, but it'll cause a whole heap of other problems. Violence has nothing to do with communication. It's not part of the negotiations that form the vast bulk of personal interaction. It's the last resort, when communication isn't an option and it's injure or be injured. Violence is what you use the moment you feel threatened.

If you realize it's possible to talk your way out of a difficult situation, that should probably be your first choice. Often, an aggressive person will put on a show to dominate without actually resorting to violence. They'll make themselves look bigger, scream obscenities or issue threats. Sometimes, they're just trying to intimidate in the hope that you'll back down. Sometimes, they're psyching themselves up for violence. You'll have to decide and act if you feel there's a real threat. Once you decide to act, act immediately.

If you don't believe a problem can be solved with language and diplomacy, say nothing. Don't look them in the eye or engage in conversation. When you enter into a conversation with a threatening person, you enter a gray zone in which it's much harder to disengage and strike the first blow. Leave if you wish to and if you can. Violence isn't always the answer, but when it is the answer, it's the only answer.

Use violence when you have no other choice. And once you start, you're not done until you finish it on your terms.

## The Reality of Violence

That's what makes it so important to know when to use your training—that's why you should only use it as an absolute last resort. You aren't trying to disable your opponent. You're using violence as a tool to cause injury. That's because if you start with the intent of causing injury, then you have a much better chance of changing the situation in your favor. You control the situation as long as you continue to injure the other guy until he's nonfunctional.

Employing social skills to handle this type of scenario puts all the control of the outcome with the guy who has the knife to your neck. This is where you need to ask yourself, "How well do I read minds?" Because you don't want to get this one wrong!

There is a big difference using social skills to assuage the ego of the guy you spilled a drink on vs. trying to use them to deal with an individual who has no problem putting a knife to your neck.

You don't need permission to use the tool of violence. It is available to you right now! The main thing I try to point out to you is you have the option to use this tool.

By learning the difference between antisocial behavior and asocial acts of violence, you end up avoiding a good deal of antisocial interactions. This by itself allows you to live a more peaceful, enjoyable life.

That's because you have no question what to do when violence is the only answer!

# Chapter Six

## Competition vs. Destruction

*"Thus the metric system did not really catch on in the States, unless you count the increasing popularity of the nine-millimeter bullet."* —Dave Barry

We all know real violence when we see it: someone being shot in the head, or stabbed repeatedly, or kicked to death by a mob. We have a primal, visceral reaction to the real thing. It sickens us.

And yet, we can watch a bloody and grueling title bout with nothing but excitement, cheering for our favorite as the two fighters beat each other to the point of exhaustion.

What's going on here?

It's very simple, really, and has to do with the difference between social interaction and asocial violence.

Consider, for example, a schoolyard fight. The bully, who occupies a position of power high up on the social totem pole, is being challenged. If the kid manages to cow the bully and make him cry, the kid will gain social status while the bully will lose status. Everyone gathers around because it's important to see who will be victorious, you want to associate yourself with the winner and shun the loser.

Such an upset, such a potential drastic change in the playground pecking order, is important to witness. The outcome of this event holds many repercussions for everyone in the social order. If the bully loses, he and his toadies will see their power eroded; kids will be less likely to hand over their lunch money. The kid who bested him will be a hero and automatically rise above the bully in social regard. If the bully prevails, the status quo is not only maintained, but reinforced. Once again, it's extremely important, as a member enmeshed in this social order, to witness the contest and its outcome.

But what about a school shooting? No one gathers around to watch that. That's because a shooting is inherently asocial, that is, we instantly recognize that it has nothing to with communication and there will be no change in the social order. There will only be mayhem, death, and misery. As such it holds no interest for the witnesses; it holds only terror.

This is what I mean when I speak of a divide between social aggression and asocial violence. They are two very different interactions with very different expected outcomes. And confusing one for the other can get you killed.

Another way of looking at it: one is a competition while the other is only about destruction. Competitions have rules. Destruction is just about who gets it right first.

Think about it—how does what you use from (insert chosen combat sport or martial art here) compare against, say, a guy trying to brain you with a tire iron (violence)?

If your response produced an injury, then wherever you got your info is irrelevant. It worked and you survive! Who cares if it was learned from combat sport X or martial art Y. What matters is, it worked within the standard of violence.

But most of the time, that isn't the case. The problem of attempting to train for competition is that it severely affects your ability to cause destruction.

For the purposes of achieving ranks, winning tournaments, and bettering your athletic skills—competition is the way to go. It takes tremendous dedication and discipline to go through the ranks and compete against other world-class athletes in your chosen sport/art.

But surviving asocial criminal violence is different. Here you must harness the power of destruction. Violence is about shutting down the human body, not scoring more points or making the other guy submit. You need to know the weak areas of the human body and how to use your brain to command the 'tools' you choose to destroy the target area and get an injury. You then continue this simple process until the other guy is nonfunctional.

The thing that is so disturbing to the competition crowd is this: many highly skilled combat sport/martial arts athletes are murdered by less athletically skilled (and often untrained) individuals.

Does that mean the competition crowd is "weaker" than the destruction crowd? No—they just are using different methods. What's important is understanding which method is appropriate to a given situation.

## Why Violence Isn't Competition

Why is it that the violence you see on the news never looks like a sparring match? Where is the back-and-forth, the cool techniques? Why is it always one guy (or guys) doing it to another guy? Why doesn't the guy taking the beating fight back?

If the true nature of violence is one person doing it to another, knocking them down and then stomping them on the ground, why does most modern martial arts and combat sports training look nothing like what you see on the news?

The answer comes down to 'The Rules.'

In the ring, the goal is to score points and get your opponent to submit, using everything allowed in the rules. Things that are against the rules are usually awful anyway: eye gouging, throat stomping, groin kicking and other 'low blows' and 'cheap shots.' We can't have these if we want to keep competition fair—if we want the winner to be the one with the most skill, strength and heart. After all, one 'cheap shot' could make it so a smaller, untrained man could win, because no one can handle losing an eye.

On the street, however, 'low blows' and 'cheap shots' are where people start—and finish —violence. It's as if they've thrown The Rules out the window and refuse to play by any rules at all. The average criminal is just not interested in competition or 'winning' in the way we like to think of it. The average criminal is interested in only one thing: taking people out.

This is why untrained criminals can take out highly trained Black Belts. The Black Belt spent most, if not all, of his time training for competition, getting stronger, learning new techniques and working very hard in the ring: in other words, following the Rules the entire time. The criminal, on the other hand, didn't train and probably couldn't name a single rule. All he knows is that if you stab someone in the neck, they tend not to get back up.

When they meet each other on the street, where there are no rules, the Black Belt is in serious trouble because he's used to playing by The Rules. In fact, The Rules have always protected him from harm. In the ring his opponent was never allowed to stab him in the neck. But outside the ring, anything goes. And the only person who is used to that lack of rules is the criminal. Someone's going to get stabbed in the neck—and I bet you can guess who it is.

If you use destruction in a competition environment, you'll be disqualified and have little chance of advancing in your chosen martial art or combat sport career. No one will want to train you or work out with you, and you'll find yourself blackballed from combat sport competitions.

On the other hand, use competition skills in a destruction environment and you have a good chance ending up maimed, crippled, or killed. If you think you can somehow switch between competition and destruction, don't be surprised if you find yourself on the highway littered with the maimed, crippled, and killed who also thought that way.

Here are the steps you need to take if you don't want it to be you:

- Make sure your training looks just like the news
- Make sure your training works when The Rules are not in play
- Make sure your training includes all the 'low blows' and 'cheap shots.'

Does your training cover all three of these? Be honest with yourself—lying about it can get you killed. If the answer is 'yes,' then you're learning 'effective self-defense' that will work anywhere, at any time. If the answer is 'no,' you'll do just fine in the ring—but what about everywhere else?

### Going Against the Rules: Using the 31 Ultimate Fighting Championship Fouls as the Basis for Operational Success in Violence

Believe it or not, most of the 31 UFC fouls are excellent guides as to what you should do in a violent situation. There are a few exceptions (a few are iffy, and two are flat-out wrong), but in general, to survive a violent situation, you need to go against the rules.

Before you cringe at the following no-holds-barred consideration of violence, remember that we are talking here about a life-or-death situation—one from which all other options have been removed. At that point, your goal is survival, and you'll do whatever it takes to live.

Of the 31 fouls, these are the ones that stand out as a blueprint for what to do—and what not to do—in violent conflict:

### Definite Yeses

1. Eye gouging of any kind. One of the three targets that do not require body weight to injure. Don't avoid this because some silly "rule" says not to.

2. Hair pulling. See 12, below.

3.  Groin attacks of any kind. The second of three that do not require body weight.

4.  Putting a finger into any orifice or into any cut or laceration on an opponent. By itself, this is just discomfort. But if we take it to mean 'rolling him over with his broken elbow' then I'm all for it.

5.  Small joint manipulation. As long as this is really code for 'breaking fingers,' I'm all for it. Personally, if I were going to use code I'd say something like 'forcible removal of all future piano concertos.'

6.  Striking to the spine or the back of the head. This is going straight for the central nervous system. Serious, life-long disability or death could result from head or spine trauma. Such things are undesirable in the ring (that's why they have a rule making it off-limits) but can mean the difference between life and death on the street.

7.  Striking downward using the point of the elbow. This is contraindicated due to 'accidental' body weight transfer. Downward means gravity-assisted, which means falling body weight; using the elbow rather than the lower arm or hand means the removal of muscle power. This changes it from a punch to a body-weighted strike. The point of the elbow is the smallest, hardest striking surface. Add it all up and you have people 'accidentally' doing an ideal strike. Line it up with a target (oh, like the spine or neck of a grounded man) and you have a guaranteed fight-ender.

8.  Throat strikes of any kind, including, without limitation, grabbing the trachea. The last of the 'Anti-Wrasslin Trifecta'. No body weight required to cause a serious injury.

9.  Clawing, pinching or twisting the flesh. By itself, this does not make the cut, as it's simply painful. As an adjunct to something vicious (like a throw or joint break) it's wonderful.

To the trained operator the human body is like a jumpsuit with handles all over it. Except that the handles are all sewn into the bones.

10. Grabbing the clavicle. See above. By itself this is merely painful. It only really becomes useful if you look at the clavicle as a handle on the battering ram you're going to try to splinter the door with—if by 'battering ram' you mean 'head' and by 'door' you mean planet Earth.

11. Kicking the head of a grounded opponent.

12. Kneeing the head of a grounded opponent.

13. Stomping a grounded opponent. Again, the 'accidental' inclusion of body weight, driven home by leg-strength and front-ended by a part of your body that's meant for rough business (your foot). Could result in actual, fight-ending injury.

14. Kicking to the kidney with the heel. Your doctor would tell you to never, ever do this. A ruptured kidney is no joke—which makes it a huge advantage in a life-or-death situation.

15. Spiking an opponent to the canvas on his head or neck. Again, 9 out of 10 doctors scream 'NO.' Especially if by 'canvas' you mean 'mall parking lot'.

16. Throwing an opponent out of the ring or fenced area. Okay, bear with me on this one. I take it to mean 'throwing into a not-nice place' like a fire hydrant or a plate glass window. Or into traffic. I'm not joking.

17. Holding the shorts or gloves of an opponent. Falls under the aegis of 4, 12 & 13, above. Useless in isolation, brilliant in conjunction with a throw.

18. Engaging in an unsportsmanlike conduct that causes an injury to an opponent. Goes without saying.

19. Holding the ropes or the fence. Typically employed when stomping or kicking a downed man. Adds leverage and improves follow-through.

20. Attacking an opponent on or during the break.

21. Attacking an opponent who is under the care of the referee.

22. Attacking an opponent after the bell has sounded the end of the period of unarmed combat. AKA 'attacking unexpectedly'. But isn't that the best time?

23. Flagrantly disregarding the instructions of the referee. Violence is the time to jettison those pesky social mores. You are free to do as you will, beholden only the physical laws of the universe.

24. Interference by the corner. Yes, your mates are free to pitch in. Many hands make light work, and all that.

## IFFY

25. Butting with the head. Goes without saying. Can it work? Sure. Ask a Scotsman ... from a distance. Is it a good idea? Hardly.

26. Biting. Three little words: BLOOD-BORNE PATHOGENS. Can it work? Sure. As an omega option. I bet you ten bucks you can figure out something better to do first.

27. Fish hooking. I actually know a guy who was in a headlock and went for the eyes and missed and ended up fish hooking the perp instead. It did make the perp let go. This is anecdotal and your mileage may vary. The danger of getting your fingers chewed on should dissuade you.

28. Spitting at an opponent. If we mean the ol' sand in the eyes trick, then maaaybe. Still, I bet you can come up with something better.

29. Timidity, including, without limitation, avoiding contact with an opponent, intentionally or consistently dropping the mouthpiece or faking an injury. This one's iffy. I take it to mean 'social manipulation to gain advantage' (see 25-27, above). But that would only really apply in antisocial situations, wouldn't it?

## FLAT-OUT NO WAY

30. Using abusive language in the ring or fenced area. Once you break that plane and cross over into violence, there is no communication.

31. Throwing in the towel during competition. You quit, you die. End of story.

The point is, real violence isn't a game. Real violence breaks all the rules. That means you'd better be ready to break them, too.

### Not All Killers Are Quitters

Most of what goes on in martial arts and combat sports works because people quit. They quit because it hurts, or because they're exhausted, or because they start to listen to the little voice that's telling them everything will be a lot better if they'd just give in and give up. More often than not it's a combination of all these things, at once; the question gets asked often enough, with each blow, "Why don't you just quit?" until they hit that personal threshold and just can't take any more.

Any technique that isn't about career-ending, crippling injury is about compliance, about making the person submit. Convincing them to quit. This is fine when the outcome isn't critical, when what happens next is nice and social. It's great for competition and the dojo. In fact, without this, sport becomes impossible without sickening 'accidents'; the dojo runs out of students as they succumb, one by one, to the brutal endpoint of their training.

Relying on your ability to make people quit, to have a higher pain tolerance, better conditioning and an indomitable will—to outlast your foe while working him to the point where he caves—will get you killed in the place where those things don't matter. If your would-be murderer is a quitter at heart, chances are you'll be fine. But if he isn't ... if he doesn't care about pain, or how tired he is, and he lacks that little voice that the sane call caution, well, he's not going to quit. Unless you know how to remove choice from the equation, he's going to kill you. Even if it takes him a little bit of work to get you there.

If he's a killer, he knows it's not about making you quit. He knows it's not about technique, or speed, or strength. It's about results. He won't waste his time engaging or setting you up. He'll go straight for those results, breaking you, shutting you down to the point where there's nothing you can do—not even quit—he'll remove choice from the equation and treat you like meat to be butchered.

Your only hope is to know how to get those results, too; to know why those results happen so you can make them happen every single time, and get it done first. Toughness, bravado, ego, superior technique—these things mean nothing in violence. Going against a killer when the prize is your life is no time to hope for the best with a suitcase full of techniques you don't fully understand—techniques that you hope will work but can't articulate why they do. If you don't know, with surety, the result you're going to get, and why that result occurs, you're out of your league when it comes to violence. And in violence there are only two kinds of people: those who know what they're doing—precisely—and the dead.

## The Terror of Competition, the Pleasure of Predation

A man approaches you on the street with a proposition: "See that guy over there?" He indicates a big, strapping fellow, his 6'4" frame enrobed in 300 lbs. of muscle. "He's coming over here to wrestle you to the ground and choke you out for a million dollars. If you can pin him instead, I'll give you the million."

"B-but," you stammer, "I don't want to wrestle him!"

The man sniffs. "Doesn't matter—he wants the million. Here he comes—best of luck!"

How does it feel to suddenly have this contest thrust upon you? To have to worry about your performance, and how it will stack up to his experience level? For all you know, he could be very good at wrestling—and even if you, yourself, are no slouch in the ring, he's clearly way outside your weight class. And much, much stronger. As he begins to sprint toward you, you notice he's a lot faster, too.

How's it feel now?

Let's try a different tack:

Same set up, except the man says, "All you have to do is touch him, and I'll give you the million instead."

Feel any different?

How about if we qualify that touch a bit—"All you have to do is break something inside of him." And you'll get the million.

In the first case, the contest is sprung upon you, you're not prepared, you're being asked to compete with the man's physical size and athletic ability. You're being asked to perform at a level most of us can't reach. You're being asked to compete in such a way that is clearly unfair, and puts you at a disadvantage.

We could just as easily set up a scenario where you are suddenly tasked with debating international monetary policy, before an audience, with someone who may or may not be a Nobel laureate in economics. We've all got the basic tools, the components to compete in such a contest—we can speak out loud, we have experience with finances and money in general—and yet, the idea makes me sweat. Most of us can expect to get hammered and humiliated, everything we say twisted back on us with a sneer and derisive laughter from the audience.

In the second case where, "All you have to do is touch him," there is no performance pressure—we can all reach out and touch the guy, even if he wants to wrestle us. In fact, there's really no way you can lose—how can he wrestle you down & choke you out without you touching him at some point? It's so simple it's ridiculous.

And sure, that 'touch' can easily be used to break something inside of him, as in the slightly more difficult scenario. We all know he can't successfully wrestle you without you crushing his groin or gouging an eye at some point. Everything he would want to do just pulls you in nice and close to those delicate anatomical features. Another easy win.

All of the above highlights another distinct difference between competition and violence—that impending competition brings with it performance anxiety as you realize you will be required to pit your skill against unknown thresholds (what if he's the better wrestler? or speaker?). It's the worry that your meager skills will be outclassed.

When we remove the competition and go instead to a win condition that is not dependent on unknown thresholds (e.g., nothing about the other guy factors into the equation) there is no dread or anxiety.

Now, I know what you're thinking—what about performance anxiety around getting violence done? Well, how anxious did you feel about merely touching the guy, above? Really? Outside of counting coup, did your anxiety increase when it was qualified as causing an injury ("...break something inside of him.")? If the answer is yes, then you're still looking at violence as competition.

Violence, as the absence of competition, has no performance anxiety component. It really is just touching, if we mean it in the same way that we would smash a soda can flat, or slam a car door, or break a stick on the curb. The physics and biomechanics involved are all the same. Any considerations beyond that are imaginary. Hang ups, if you will.

As with pretty much everything in this work, the solution is mat time. It's the second best place to learn that competition has nothing to do with anything in violence, that size, speed and strength have no bearing on who wins and who dies. Those who still view violence as a form of competition, a high-stakes one, act hesitantly on the mats; they keep their distance (even when they think they're penetrating), flinch, hide and otherwise give poor reactions, and rarely employ body weight. They behave as if they are fundamentally frightened of what's going on. Which they are.

Those who have figured it out by physically burning the idea out of their heads with hours of mat time throw themselves into the work with great relish, applying themselves bodily to every problem presented them. The physical realization that violence is about a failure to compete, an end-run around competition, is liberating. Gone is the worry about being big enough, fast enough or strong enough. The other guy's skill counts for absolutely nothing. It's all about you, and only you. The other guy is prey to be taken, meat to be butchered. The pressure's off and you're free to do as you will. You're exercising your legacy as a predator—and by all accounts, predation is pleasurable.

# Chapter Seven

## All The Reasons Why You Can't

No sane person wants to be involved in violence. If you did, all you'd have to do is run outside your house and punch the first person you saw in the neck as hard as you could. Getting involved in a violent act is easy. The fact that you don't go looking for it is a testament to your civility, sociability, and sanity. Everybody's willing to cop to this.

But there's something more than basic humanity underlying your aversion to violence. I'm sure that if you sat down right now and made yourself a list of the top twenty reasons you don't want to get into a violent encounter, one or two would result from civility and the others would all come from the same source: fear. All of those excuses come down to the same thing: you are afraid of violence.

Now, don't take that the wrong way. There's nothing wrong with being afraid—a little fear is healthy, and to paraphrase Eddie Rickenbacker, America's top fighter ace in WWI, there is no courage without fear. What's wrong is lying to yourself about it. You come up with all the reasons you can't engage in violence, but what they really are is a smokescreen designed to protect your ego from becoming aware that you're scared. And there's a problem with lying to yourself: deep down, you know the truth. You're not actually saving your ego from anything, because you know you're lying to yourself inside.

But with a little effort and a lot of time, you can usually succeed in convincing your conscious mind that you're telling the truth— that it doesn't come down to fear but a host of other excuses. Sometimes it takes an outside source pointing out those fears before your conscious mind jibes with your unconscious and realizes the truth. So finally, collected in a single place (other than the inside of your skull), here are all the reasons why you can't—and the truth behind them!

## Physical Excuses

### 1. I Don't Have Enough Training! *"I take classes in self-defense/martial arts/fighting, but I don't have enough days/months/years/belts/levels to be able to hurt someone."*

If only you had more time in, you'd be ready. Maybe next month. Maybe next year. The sad part is you typically don't get to pick when violence happens, so you're as ready as you're ever gonna be. Wouldn't it be nice if you could stop a criminal in his tracks and say, "Sorry, pal, I'm not ready for this yet. Can you come back in a few months?" You can't. And the fact that most people who successfully use violence (incarcerated criminals) have little or no training whatsoever blows this one out of the water.

### 2. I'm Not Coordinated!

I hear it all the time: "I can't move like you guys do!" Neither could Frank the Lawyer, the self-proclaimed Most Uncoordinated Person In The Universe. Stop me if you've heard this one before (and if you've trained with me live, you have). I trained Frank for about a year, a year spent lying awake at night agonizing over his personal safety. He was the only person I ever trained who I prayed to God would never, ever be called upon to use his training. He was the most uncoordinated person I'd ever met. He had two left feet—and that was just his hands. Fast forward five years and I get a phone call from him telling me how he took out two muggers, one of whom had a knife. And to quote him, "It was just like a movie." This was the guy who convinced me that if he can do it, literally anyone can. Scratch that excuse.

### 3.  *I'm Physically Not Able!*

The wheelchair-bound, the blind, a guy with one functional arm. What do they all have in common? Not this excuse. These are all people I trained—and they were more than capable of getting it done right. What's your excuse? A bum knee? I got two of 'em. You have no excuse. Even if it's as severe as the ones above, it didn't slow anybody I know down. It only slows you down if you want it to. Sure, there might be some challenges, but we work around them. Once you stop viewing, for example, blindness as a complete incapacitation and start seeing it as a hurdle to be overcome—just like a bad knee or a sprained elbow—you not only have what you need to start your training, you have what you need to seriously improve your entire life!

## Mental Excuses

### 4.  *I'm Not Cut Out For It!  Not cut out for violence?*

Don't be ridiculous. If you're human, you are. You're born to it, built for it, and the only reason you're here is because all your ancestors did it to everything that got in their way. If we could bring back a Neanderthal I guarantee he'd piss his hides at the mere sight of you. You might not think of yourself as particularly scary, but then you've forgotten that your kind wiped his kind out. Whether you like it or not, everyone's cut out for the commission of violence. That guy you run into on the street isn't all that scary either—in fact, if you saw him begging in an alley, you'd probably feel a combination of pity and revulsion. What makes him scary is that he has the intent of hurting you. So all you need to make yourself scary is—you got it—the exact same intent.

### 5.  *I Could Never Do That To Someone!*

Yeah, this is typically code for "Holy $#!& I had no idea people did that to each other and so I'm going to go unilateral for the peace-thing with the idea that if I don't do it to anybody then no one will ever do it to me." You'd be amazed at what you can do when the social security blanket gets stripped away and it's just the screech and sparks of your life rubbing up against the steel deck-plate of reality.

A gentleman once openly scoffed at me and said, "I could never kick someone in the throat when they were down."

Really? Not even if they were down because they were picking up a gun to shoot you with? You really are very sporting about your own murder. Closed-casket funeral notwithstanding.

What he was really saying was that he was afraid. As we all are. But he was lying to me about it, as if I wouldn't notice, and worst of all, he was lying to himself. What's that? You think maybe he wasn't afraid, but just valued fair play? Well, we all do. That's normal. But the point I keep trying to drive home is that a real violent situation has nothing to do with fair play. It's not a game, and if you try to observe the rules of polite society, you're not "valuing fair play"—you're making an egotistical statement about how much better you are than that criminal. Unfortunately, in this case, your statement won't matter much to your grieving family at your funeral.

So this man's statement isn't about his morality, it's about his fear and egoism. If he's lucky, it'll never matter. And statistics are on his side. If he ain't lucky, that ego's gonna get him killed. And for no good reason other than he was unwilling to admit a small, universal weakness.

## Fear and Courage

I have to tell you, Rickenbacker's quote startled me. I mean, he was the top American ace in WWI. He once dove on and single-handedly fought with a formation of seven planes. Seven to one, by choice. A stone-to-the-bone killer. And he admitted to spending most of his time terrified out of his gourd. But then, as he said, "there is no courage without fear."

So get over it. You have no excuse. You're not saying you can't, you're saying you don't want to. Well, none of us do.

Train hard, to the best of your abilities and know that it's more than enough. It's served people who were smaller than you, weaker than you, less well trained than you, when it counted most. And they've all made it back alive and well. So can you. But only if you quit with the excuses and get to work.

## Filthy Lies

Every now and again something gets stuck in my craw, jammed in there so tight that the only things that're going to get it out are a tire iron and a liberal dose of bile. Here's a dose of both for three things that got stuck in there recently—lies I hear people tell themselves and each other about training for violence:

### 1. *Intellectual understanding of the material is key.*

The criminal sociopath knows only one thing about violence—that the person doing it wins. And even that statement is too wordy. That's not to say the average criminal is stupid. It's just that violence operates where intellect stops coming into play—in other words, from a gut level of what you have to do to survive. That's why you'll never hear a criminal use the words I just did, even though if you said it to them, they'd agree it was true. When asked to articulate what works in violence they'll tend to speak to injuries—you know, things like "What works? Knee 'em in the groin/stab 'em in the neck/shoot 'em in the head."

Intellectual discourse on the subject is an exercise for instruction, not for doing. Who actually believes that a football team would be better off if they spent every practice talking about football instead of actually playing football? Your best bet for getting good at violence is to practice doing it—not sit around talking about it. You should really only be sitting down and talking about it because you're wiped out from practicing so damn much.

## 2. Once the technique is automatic, it will take care of everything.

No, it won't. Either you're going to take care of it, or nothing's going to happen. 'Doing a technique' is like throwing a hood ornament at someone—when what you really want to do is hit them with a truck that just happens to have a hood ornament bolted on the front end.

Knowing how to set up a specific joint break is not the same thing as breaking a joint. Likewise, knowing the precise 'hand wave' to 'claw the eyes' is not the same as causing a serious eye injury. A subtle distinction? It has to do with how far into/through the other man you're thinking. A typical technique stops at the outer boundary of your skin—it's a subjective, personal exercise that has very little to do with the Other Guy or even realistic results. You know what it's supposed to do, but because technique focuses primarily on hand waving and foot placement there's really no way to be sure of the outcome.

Breaking out beyond technique means looking through an anatomical feature in him and converting it into an unrecognizable mess. It's starting with the result you need—injury—and working backwards from there to figure out how to get that result. Or, to put it another way, technique is like obsessively polishing an empty gun. What you want to do instead is study gunshot wounds and figure out how best to make those.

In other words, techniques only work when they ... well, work! To stick with the idea of the football team: sure, there might be some value in the team meeting, where they have a

49

brief discussion of strategy. But do they then go home and work through the motions of that strategy on their own? Of course not! They have a team practice, a scrimmage game, and put those principles into motion exactly how they'll do it in the real game. That's where technique falls apart and actual real-life practice takes over.

### 3.  *I can't be expected to do it because I'm not ready.*

You're half right. You won't be able to do it until you give yourself permission to be ready. The only gatekeeper holding you back here is you. So why not take the time, like, right now, and decide that you can for a change?

It's shockingly easy to blind a man, make him barf his own nuts, bust his leg and stomp on his neck to end him. The only thing missing is your full force and effort, the physical symptom of a little something we call intent, and that's just you giving yourself permission to do what your inner predator wants to do anyway.

"I'm not ready" is kung-fu theater bullshit. It's a responsibility dodge. What you're really saying is, "I don't want to be responsible for screwing up. I want to be able to blame the training." You gotta wake up and own it. You gotta take responsibility for what you know and what that makes you. To do otherwise is to let yourself down—it's participating in your own murder.

Have you ever watched sumo wrestlers—you know, the huge guys who look like they're wearing diapers? An actual sumo match is very brief, but the build-up can take forever. That's because it doesn't start until both wrestlers indicate that they're ready by placing their knuckles on the white line. Sometimes for up to ten minutes, one or both wrestlers approach the line, squat down, get up, and walk away while their opponent patiently waits for that signal.

That's why sumo wrestling is not violence. No criminal will

patiently wait until you're ready, and if you expect him to, you're going to get yourself killed.

To be honest, nobody's ready; nobody wants to go there. But the last thing you want when you do end up there is to be dragging a big heavy sack of self-doubt along for the ride.

Everything outside of the mechanical facts of injury—body weight driven through vulnerable anatomy—is an illusion.

# Chapter Eight

## Spiritual Enlightenment, Competition and the One-Way Street of Violence

Violence is eons older than polite society. It had long been the dominant tool of last resort before anything even remotely human strode the savannah. And that worked fine as long as we were dealing with animals with two primary objectives: survive and establish dominance. But once we were here, and began to pull together and organize against this hostile environment we call home, it became crucial to put limits on violence within society. After all, you can't build a pyramid if everyone's busy choking each other out.

We added rules, decided society-by-society when it was appropriate and when it was not, who could do it to whom, and the state-sanctioned use of the tool on those who broke the rules. This is not a bad thing. This is the necessary order of history.

Violence, then, gave rise to traditional martial arts, which in turn produced combat sports. Makes sense, right?

It's not so clear-cut to everyone. If I had a steel penny for every time I've heard someone refer to TFT training as being just like this or that martial art or a 'really brutal' version of combat sports, I'd be able to fire torpedoes full of cash down on Bill Gates' head from my solid-gold orbital rail gun. (Do you have any idea how much it costs to get solid-gold I-beams into orbit? Neither do I).

Because the family tree goes:

*Rock to the Head*  ⇨  *Crane Style*  ⇨  *Wrestling Match*

and not the other way around, this view is a funny one.

TFT is not the next step in the evolution of modern martial arts; it's a return to the root of the whole matter. 'Back to basics,' if you will. In other words, I'm not trying to teach you anything new. In fact, I'm trying to work all of those newfangled (if you can count something society came up with a couple thousand years ago as "new") rules and ideas out of your head and get you back to what your basic instincts already know: the primary, raw rush of violence in its coldest, most brutal form.

## Martial Arts: An Empty Bottle of Violence With a Child-Proof Cap

Long ago, the martial arts were the initial attempt to codify and keep knowledge of violence to train elite troops. In other words, Asian societies used martial arts to train warriors. The original martial arts were limited to a select warrior elite, and they had one objective: to train people in the effective use of violence. As time went on, though, warfare stopped being about physical ability and became more and more about weapons. The warrior elite vanished and the martial arts began to open to anyone who displayed an interest. As the schools got further and further from that original purpose—training for war—the teaching was more and more diluted with philosophy and religion. As well it should be—it wasn't necessarily a good idea to train the average person in the skills of total war.

Instead, martial arts staked a claim to the foggy gray expanse of the antisocial realm—how to behave when dealing with social belligerents. Or, more plainly, how to be the best damn bar-fighter to ever sit a stool.

This is the area that martial arts is famous for: how do I deal with a drunk?

It all starts with a bunch of rules on social decorum—essentially a checklist of social tools to try and defuse the antisocial bomb. When all that has been tried, and failed, then comes the fighting stance and perhaps a verbal warning. This is the equivalent of the frightened cat arching its back and hissing in an attempt to look threatening. Then comes blocking, and 'techniques' designed to convince the unruly to quit: punches, kicks, joint-locking, etc.

For the most part, it works. Martial arts has taken ownership of the antisocial realm and worked very hard to give practitioners a road map to navigate all the pitfalls and mine fields. And if the situation truly is antisocial in nature, blocking, punches, kicks, joint locking, etc., work well. But when we move from antisocial behavior to asocial behavior ... well, that's where martial arts start to lose their grip.

## Combat Sports: Violence Made Palatable

Thanks to the Internet, things we couldn't have imagined seeing fifty years ago are now readily available. In the sixties, it was astonishing to people to see a man walk on the moon. With the internet, though, you can get all kinds of visual media, things that used to be forbidden or at least damn difficult to get your hands on— like video clips of unrestrained violence. There is, however, little interest in such things. Sane people cannot stomach real violence— we literally have a gut reaction to it. And it's unpleasant.

Movies that attempt to recreate real-world violence—with an unflinching eye and no stylistic embellishments—make people leave the theater.

But what if we could make violence palatable? What if we could titillate and tease with just enough action to excite the predator within us all while maintaining enough padding to keep from scaring the higher-order functions?

Let's say we put rules on it and make it a contest of strength, skill and will instead of maiming and killing. I bet people would pay money to see that.

And they do.

But still we're sickened when someone actually breaks an arm, or loses an eye.

That's because obvious, crippling injury is coloring outside the lines—it's not social anymore. As long as we can all enjoy the sensation of watching the school-yard tussle without crossing over into the school-yard shooting, we'll pay to play. And that's where combat sports come in.

Want a prime example? Wrestling has been a ratings jackpot for decades now on prime time television. Everyone knows it's fake. That's why we're appalled when someone actually gets hurt: this is a game, and we don't expect actual injuries from a game. We might think we're witnessing violence, but even while we get a vicarious thrill, the human inside us knows that we're playing by an established set of rules, and it reacts with shock and horror when those rules are violated.

### Violence: Not Just 'Anything Goes' but 'Do Your Worst'

What we strive to teach you with TFT is not just martial arts knobbed up to 11 or combat sports without the rules—it's to get back to the genesis of all the rest of that stuff. It's back to basics.

When people think of violence as martial arts gone wild, they are trying to drag an antisocial tool into the asocial realm. To be metaphorical, it's like trying to use a can opener to change a tire on a car: wrong tool for the job. To be more concrete, it's like putting out your hand and shouting "No!" to dissuade a sociopath from killing you.

Wrong tool for the job, indeed.

When people think of violence as combat sports 'without the rules,' they're also missing the point. Again, they're thinking of violence as 'anything goes' when really it's 'do your worst.' While it sounds like pencil-necked semantics, it's really a chilling distinction.

'Anything goes' means you can do anything, and when left

to their own devices people will choose non-awful things. Innate squeamishness will keep sane people away from the eyes, as in periorbital scratching, where people who were being strangled to death, murdered, choose to scratch at the eyes rather than dig them out. What other situation, outside of your own murder, could be more 'anything goes?'

Violence, on the other hand, is 'do your worst,' as in 'go to the end of the list and pick the most god-awful thing—and start there.' It means you will start by taking the man's eye, then break his leg to drop him and stomp him like you're making an apocalyptic vintage from the grapes of wrath. No ifs, ands, or buts, no veering off from the socially unacceptable, the horrible, or the sickening. In point of fact those things are your stock in trade. They are the tools you use, not 'techniques.'

The key difference here between "anything goes" and "do your worst" is this: with "anything goes," you start small and work up. With "do your worst," you start with the worst possible injury you can inflict. And that makes the difference between pissing your attacker off and incapacitating him.

In violence you don't best the man or even win—you do horrible, sickening, awful things to him. You do them first, without hesitation and without stopping out of pity or horror.

Is it really any wonder, then, that our ancestors sought to minimize and hobble violence with social constraints, limits and rules?

## How Much Philosophy In A Bullet?

People like to get philosophical about hand-to-hand combat. Dueling, martial arts, swordplay—all traditions deeply woven with aphorisms, exhortations, rules and other philosophical constructs. Why, then, does no one wax poetic for handguns?

guided practice.

This is the crux of my argument, and cannot be overstated. Much of the time I see philosophy used as a buffer between the practitioner and what has to be done. Accepting the biomechanical reality of it is far more important than any feeling of moral superiority. The stark white light of what is required—force and a target, a bullet in a brain—burns away the extraneous junk.

Once you know how to hurt people, you're free to think of it however you wish (although I've found that most people are unwilling to add superfluous adornments once they really grok what we're up to. Stapling the Mona Lisa to a supermodel improves neither).

### Problems with Philosophy from a Perspective Within Violence

It's actually very simple to sum up the problems with mixing philosophy and violence. Philosophy is:

1. *Not part of the definition of violence*

2. *Subjective*

3. *A social construct.*

Only two elements are required for injury: large amounts of kinetic energy and human tissue. The gun is the perfect tool to illustrate this. The bullet is pushed out of the gun and flies away with a big, fat load of kinetic energy—if it hits a piece of a human being, it's going to wreck it.

Where is the philosophy? Nowhere to be found. It can exist before the trigger pull and then later in the hospital, but for the moment when the bullet cuts a trajectory through a target there is none. And as we've established previously, if it's not necessary for injury, it's worthless. No matter how much you might wish it were so, a philosophical stance cannot break a knee (or prevent your knee from breaking).

Philosophy is purely subjective. What is profound and illuminating for one person is the inane natterings of the Cult of Hogwash for another. I will never tell you how I order the skill of hurting people for me, in my life. I would expect what works for me to be meaningless to you. And I am not so egocentric to believe otherwise. If we had a standard TFT philosophical line, we would alienate some percentage of potential clients right out of the gate. It's more important that everyone develops their own approach that works for them.

Philosophy is a social construct. And yet, violence is asocial. Sounds pretty damn incompatible to me. There is no good or evil in violence—only success and failure. Philosophy is after the fact and typically involves a cup of hot cocoa. And a comfy chair. It would cease to exist, momentarily, if you threw your boiling hot cocoa into someone's face, broke their leg and stomped on their throat. It would then come back into being again, informing the judge's decision on whether or not to give you the gas chamber.

Violence is biomechanical. It requires nothing—nothing—but force and a target. Period. Anything that pulls you away from this reality is window dressing, padding, blinders and earplugs. Anything between you and this fact is an obstacle that you must overcome in order to act.

## Psychic Oven Mitts

So what good is philosophy then? Philosophical precepts and their more formal, ritual expression—religion—typically inform a person about their place in the universe and what constitutes acceptable (and unacceptable) social behavior. Or, more simply, how we relate to the universe and how we relate to each other. The first case is way out of bounds for this discussion. The second case, how we relate to each other, would seem to govern violence. It does, but only before and after the act. It does nothing to bolster your chances of success in the moment of violence.

Because, quite frankly, philosophy does not exist in the moment of violence. No more than it exists in bullets. Philosophy is for getting a handle on what your skill-set means to you: when and how to use it. But the skill-set is still the skill-set. Like a gun, how you think about it doesn't change the reality of it. The only thing we can show you how to do is hurt people.

I do believe that it is imperative that each practitioner come to grips with this in their own way—I especially recommend that they work it into their previously chosen ethical framework rather than making up or adopting new ones; new or novel philosophy that is ungrounded in your religious or life experience will infect and insinuate itself into your training, tainting the biomechanical purity of hurting people. In other words, the philosophy becomes a part of the tool rather than merely informing your use of it.

You have to think of it this way: we all know that in any religion, some prayers get answered and some don't. So would you rather see each bullet as a prayer to the Death God or as simple physics, kinetic energy striking matter?

Philosophy can get you to the point of pulling the trigger and can help you order and understand what you've done after the fact, but it has nothing to do with the biomechanical realities of violence and can, in fact, act as an impediment to success in both learning and doing violence.

What serves you best is to view violence in purely biomechanical terms. Learn it in a philosophically sterile, asocial environment. Once you got hurting people down cold, look to your own heart to find what that means for you.

# Chapter Nine

## Stripping the Fat to Find the Bone — Reason in Violence

Sane, well-socialized people see violence as insane. When we hear about violence, we're usually talking about terrorists, criminals, sociopaths—in other words, horrible events perpetrated by horrible, mentally unstable people. By saying you are willing to use violence as a survival tool you are also saying (in the layperson's mind) that you are a card-carrying member of one of the groups above.

Sane, well-socialized people want desperately to ascribe 'reason' to violence. That's because violence is a scary, random thing that they (typically) only ever think of as happening to someone else. If they can hitch it to a reason, then they think they can use their social skills to avoid it by:

- Staying out of 'bad' parts of town.
- Being nice to people.
- Avoiding the insane.

Not bad ideas in general, but hardly enough insurance for you, personally, to bet the rest of your life on. 'Speak softly but carry a big stick' and all that. The essential problem is that when the layperson looks at the idea of violence without reason they see (rightfully so) the very definition of a monster. And so, when you say you're willing to use real, hardcore, brutal violence, in their eyes you've just exposed yourself as a monster.

They don't understand that a tool is just a tool. Picking up and using a hammer to drive nails doesn't mean you're any more likely to run around the neighborhood smashing car windows than you were before you picked it up. Of course, the layperson sees an increased likelihood of vandalism simply because you picked up the tool. They suffer from an underlying assumption that there is reason and purpose to it—you only ever pick up a hammer to nail things, right?

For a sane, well-socialized person who happens to be trained in the use of violence as a survival tool, you are no more likely to use it inappropriately, in monstrous fashion, than you were before you were trained. In fact, you're probably less likely to seek out 'opportunities' to use it now that you know, without ambiguity, what's at stake. (Nobody's willing to die for a parking space—unless you live in Southern California).

People who really understand violence, rather than just viewing it from the fringes, know that it's no more or less a tool than the hammer. Violence isn't right or wrong—where and how you choose to use it is. But it is this dispassionate, morally-neutral view of violence that is troubling to the average person. There has to be reason behind it, passionate and evil, or there is no social blanket woven of rules thick enough to keep them warm against the shuddering cold void of the universe laid bare.

What they need to understand is that we use violence when our long utility belt of shopworn 'social' tools fail to get the job done. The tool of violence is only good for one thing—shutting off a human brain. It's the end of the line, the final option in a long list of tools and techniques. If you're injuring people, you've run through and exhausted all the other 'social' tools and arrived at the last one, glinting cold and hard in its 'in case of emergency break things' box.

I do not use violence out of anger. This is not a requirement for injury. That also scares people, who think violence is an irrational act and should therefore be committed in an irrational state of mind. In fact, killing with dispassion is the hallmark of the sociopath. This is the stickiest point for most people—they assume that if you don't have to be 'worked up' in order to injure people then you're empty inside, too.

Violence is not insanity, either. If you were sane before you understood violence, you'd still be you on the other side. 'Crazy' is also not a requirement for injury.

The simple fact is that there is no reason to it. You're not injuring someone because of any extraneous reason—you're injuring them to shut them off. If you're in there to 'fight for your life' and he's just in it to kill you, you're probably going to get killed. The person with the clearest, cleanest and smallest achievable goal will tend to prevail. This is what I mean when I say 'intent,' which is another way of expressing monomaniacal focus. The focusing of your entire will and effort onto one small thing at a time—destroying a single square inch of him.

This one small thing is so monumentally important I worked it into the title of what we do—Target-Focus Training

**Splitting Hairs or Splitting Heads: The Semantics of Violence**

There is nothing sexy about beating a man to death with a tire iron.

Okay, let's rewind a little bit. I had two very different (and yet not so) conversations about violence with two very different (and yet not so) individuals. The first one involved a grandmother and her very young grandson who just happened to be walking by a bunch of Mastery students savaging each other outside a Las Vegas seminar. She looked extremely uneasy, the child even more so.

"What is this?" she asked, eyes wide.

"It's the intelligent use of violence as a survival tool," I replied.

"Like self-defense? Like when you're in trouble?"

I hesitated. I wanted to say 'no, more like breaking people' but she had asked with such hope in her voice, as in, 'I sure do hope this isn't what my gut is telling me it is—please reassure me'. So I blinked and let it go.

"Yes," I said, "It's exactly like that."

Her face flushed with relief. It wasn't what the awful knot in her gut said it was. These were sane people after all.

The second conversation occurred at my son's weekly piano lesson. It turns out that I went to high school with one of the teachers, and when he realized this he Googled me to see what I'd been up to for the last twenty years.

"So, you're still doing that martial arts thing?" he asked.

"Yeah," I nodded, "except it's not martial arts."

He frowned. "So it's like self-defense?"

"No—more like beating a man to death with your bare hands."

His eyes widened and heads began to turn. The metaphorical needle came off the record and the chatter in the room dipped a bit as people began to tune in to our conversation.

"So you don't use any weapons."

Once again, the hopeful inflection in the voice. He wanted me to veer back into something sane, and away from the idea of killing.

I didn't blink. I gave it to him straight. "Sure we do—you can beat a man to death with a tire iron or stab him to death with a kitchen knife. It's all the same."

That did it. Everyone in the room was listening now. Everyone had questions, and every single one of them was to try to get me to recant, to box me into a corner where I'd have to admit that what I meant was a sane, righteous, defensive use of force to disarm or disable an 'attacker'—not the wanton misuse of power to maim, cripple and kill at will.

I was my usual courteous, approachable, informational self—

but something tells me future conversation at music class will be strained. Maybe I should have told them it was all about timeshares ...

Often, when I'm attempting to explain what it is I do, I'm accused of splitting hairs, told that it's 'all just semantics.' That one man's self-defense is another man's tire iron murder. But the ridiculousness of that sentence shows it ain't so.

I've written previously about how well-socialized humans like to fall back on euphemisms to distance themselves from the ugly, brutal reality of what has to happen in violence—namely, you seriously injuring another person. Not stopping when he begs you to stop. Not interacting with him as a person, or even an enemy, but as meat to be torn to uselessness.

Describing it in these terms causes (dare I say) violent reactions in lay people as they instantaneously judge you to be adrift without moral compass, operating at the debased level of the thug—in a word, insane.

People parse killing in socially acceptable terms (martial arts, self-defense, etc.), to show other socialized people that they are not 'bad.' When someone defies convention and steps out of bounds ('beat a man to death with a tire iron'), the strong reaction comes from an unconscious, intrinsic understanding that if everyone's playing by the same rules, we're all okay. But there's a problem with that philosophy, and it comes as soon as you encounter someone who isn't playing by those rules.

This social parsing of violence then takes the next step up to seize the moral high ground where we all have permission to behave badly. Witness the 'attacker/defender' dichotomy. If you are the defender, you are cleared, in pretty much everyone's mind, to brain the attacker.

The moral high ground is also a cool place to be seen. There you are, on the wind-swept mountain top, beams of blinding righteousness radiating from your head. It's super sexy with a double side order of pizzazz. Having a black belt in martial arts impresses friends, and whatnot. Knowing how to kill a man is less cool in most circles. Being ready and willing to do so is another thing entirely.

Maintaining righteousness in the face of simple killing takes a lot of mental gymnastics. Many people try using Animal Farm-esque stand-ins to try to illuminate roles to be played. White hats and black hats. The protectors and the helpless. Guess what? Those are nice lies we tell ourselves to feel better about what it is we're training to do.

There is no animal schema, no predator and prey, regardless of which one you think you are. There are only naked humans, milling about on an infinite gray plain. You're one of them, and everyone else is stuck there with you. We all have the same set of advantages and disadvantages. Identical physical constraints and powers. We each possess the most dangerous weapon in the universe, a human brain.

Everyone, exactly the same on a level playing field. Not comforting in the least, but then, when was the last time reality was comforting? And that's the problem: in most people's minds, there's no difference between saying, "I am able and prepared to kill someone if necessary" and saying "I'm a psychotic killer and you probably shouldn't be alone with me, especially if there's a weapon handy."

So how do we talk about it? Let's look at some of the most common terms, and then I'll toss mine in. And I promise it'll be a live psychic grenade.

## MARTIAL ARTS

This term really only works in the ancient Greek sense, as in 'the skills required by warriors to make war.' This sense has been completely lost in the modern day (think of the Olympic Decathlon), and I doubt anyone out there thought of 'maintaining and operating a cruise missile launcher' when they read the words 'martial arts.'

More likely than not you thought of your local Karate school. And until that kind of training is necessary for serial killers to ply their hobby, it will remain a misnomer for what it is I do.

## Self-Defense

This is the next logical step. And yet, 'beating a man to death with a tire iron' tends to strain the definition of self-defense beyond the breaking point. Self-defense requires an attacker; it requires you to be second-banana in physical terms (as the lowly, yet beloved defender), but don't sweat it. 'Cuz you've got the moral high ground and that awful attacker had no right to be doing these things to you. Good luck, and remember this comforting fact: you are in the right no matter how it all works out.

Beating a man to death with a tire iron probably isn't allowed in self-defense, but—funny how the universe works—it may be just the thing that has to happen in order for you to survive. And that's where the term breaks down. We can't call violence self-defense because when most people hear that term they assume you've been attacked before you did any violence of your own—and then that violence is designed not to injure, but to temporarily incapacitate your attacker long enough for you to get away. That's great, isn't it? Except what happens if there are two attackers, or three, or nine, and your attempt at incapacitation goes wrong?

When given the choice between self-defense and survival, let's all pick survival, shall we?

## Fighting

This term doesn't work because it's too wide open. You can fight with your sibling, your spouse, and your boss. On the high end you can fight for your rights; on the low end you can fight for the TV remote. Do any of these uses make you think of stabbing someone in the neck—other than the one about the TV remote?

Fights can have rules and referees. Murders don't.

**Hand-to-Hand Combat**

Here we are—down to the hard nuts, in your face, XXX-TREEEME!!! term. While on the surface it would seem to be the one we want, it's still lacking. Hand-to-hand carries with it the connotation of back-and-forth, tit-for-tat. Most people would not readily apply the label to a man being beaten to death with a tire iron. The question you have to ask yourself is: "Do the people who are best at violence in our society (the criminal sociopaths) truly engage in hand-to-hand combat?" I'll let you answer it for yourself.

So what is it I do? What words can ever truly communicate the essence of it?

At a recent seminar someone asked a question about an extremely accomplished combat-sports champion. This champion is big and tough and skilled. The question was, 'how would you defeat so-and-so?'

To which I replied, without hesitation, "I'd start by hiring someone to shoot his father."

And that's it exactly, rendered as precisely as words will allow.

# Chapter Ten

## Everyone's a Badass

Human societies are fascinated with strength and power. Obvious personal power, especially height, musculature, and a hair-trigger willingness to do violence are eternally impressive to us. Hence the rise of the "anti-hero" on television and in movies—the hero who, in reality, would be a pretty dangerous guy you wouldn't want to meet, but makes a compelling fantasy. We all desire what those attributes grant the possessor: respect, awe, and perhaps fear.

When we are intimidated, we feel all those things acutely. Most of all the gut-snarling fear. We feel it, and we want to make others feel those things, too. We feel it and realize we don't want to confront the intimidating person ... and wouldn't that feeling be a very useful thing to project? Doesn't it seem like the perfect solution? After all, if you're scary enough, no one's going to mess with you, right?

Unfortunately, that's not the case. Your brand new badass attitude is probably going to get that bad ass kicked. Intimidation is like juggling 13 double-edged swords and playing with fire simultaneously.

For our purposes I'm going to define 'intimidation' as the antisocial process of going out of your way to make someone afraid of you. Most people take this a step farther, not stopping at mere fear but going headlong into humiliation. Once they realize they've made someone afraid, they will typically push it and rub it in to humiliate the affected person.

As an interesting aside, it's a common truth that people who use intimidation as a social tool will do the things that would intimidate them—they will project the behaviors that they, themselves, fear most.

Why is intimidation so dangerous? Because whether you fail or succeed at it, it can get you killed. If you fail to intimidate the man, you have just escalated the situation—saying, in effect, "Do you want me to hurt you?"—and now, unimpressed, he's calling your bluff. If he's the kind of guy who responds to threats with physical action, then it's on. You just called it down upon yourself because you wanted to be a badass.

Most of the time it's not going to be a problem—if the badass thing went physical all the time very few people would do it, right? The problem is, the people who get set off by this are the worst kind. In other words, the sane, normal people are the ones who will get scared and back down. So who are you left with? Criminals, sociopaths, murderers... and I hope I don't have to tell you that choosing to escalate a screaming match to a life-or-death situation is asinine.

Let's say you succeed in intimidating him. Mission accomplished, right? You put him in his place; you showed him (and everyone in earshot) who's boss, you made him feel afraid. How could that possibly go wrong?

Yeah, I know—it's a rhetorical question.

Let's flip it around: he succeeded in intimidating you, he made you feel afraid. Maybe even made you feel afraid for your life. How do you respond? If you know how to handle the physical side, or are carrying a gun, you can take it there in a blink of an eye and shut him off. Maybe you just feel socially embarrassed and walk away. Or maybe you knock him down, knee him in the face and stomp on his head until he's nonfunctional. Who can say? It's going to be decided on a case-by-case basis.

So you make him feel afraid. Most people will back down and disengage, usually while making even more noise than before. But there are some, the worst out there, who will take it as a threat and work to destroy that threat. They may go off instantaneously, or they may simmer for hours, days, months. In the long-term case, you probably won't have the luxury of seeing it coming. And if you truly terrified them, they're going to want to do things to even the odds —things like coming back with accomplices and firearms.

So, succeed or fail, intimidation can get you killed. It's a sucker's game.

I can just hear you getting up in arms. Some of you believe that if you're not the intimidator, you're prey. You point to the wild and demonstrate how a lion puffs out its chest and roars to frighten off its competition, and you think you should do the same.

I've got news for you: you're not a cat. Let's make a quick clarification here: the opposite of being intimidating is not the same as appearing meek, weak or helpless—it's simply not registering as prey. Looking like you know what you're doing and know what's going on, and yet assuming a comfortably unconcerned air, is more akin to being socially remote than a badass. That is, you've got the NO SOLICITING sign out without being a jerk about it. Appearing unimpressed and unafraid is not the same as being intimidating.

You can project the confidence that you can handle yourself without threatening anyone. A high order social skill? Probably one of the highest. And for many people, elusive. But it's a lot less harrowing than running around being intimidating, which is exhausting and scary at the same time.

I think of it like this: "Go out of your way to get to the rest of your day."

When in the social arena, be social, use your social skills, and treat everyone like people. In the asocial arena treat everyone like meat. Don't confuse the two.

It doesn't mean you have to be everyone's friend, a 'pushover' or smile at daily human ugliness. It can be as simple as biting your tongue instead of spitting fuel on the fire. Of course, the hard part is if you're successful, you'll never know it. You'll never even be aware of the trouble you've dodged. You can only ever be aware of the trouble you've caused.

## Violence in the Antisocial Realm

The use of violence can have unintended consequences. Tearing into someone physically can end up killing them, even when you didn't mean to. And if it later turns out that the circumstances didn't justify that killing, you can be subject to serious legal (and life-changing) consequences down the road. These consequences are the reason I do not recommend using violence in antisocial situations—wrong tool for the job and all that. It's far better, in the short and long term, to disengage and get the hell out of there.

That's all well and good, and in a perfect world, things should be so clear-cut and easy. But we don't live in that world, and they're not. Those 'unintended consequences' cut both ways—say he just wants to 'kick your ass' and you end up brained on the sidewalk as a result. Everyone ends up sad, and he'll cry in court about how he didn't mean it, it was all a terrible mistake, his life is ruined, etc. Fat lot of good that does you.

And that's why I'll never tell you to hold back and take a beating. So the question is, how do you use violence in the antisocial arena?

The sad answer is, pretty much the same way you do in the asocial arena. You need to break things inside of him so they don't work anymore. There are a couple of important ideas you need to understand, and keep in mind, if you're going to use that stick of dynamite to open your car door, after all:

### 1. Don't pull any punches.

You cannot 'go easy' on him just because this started out as an antisocial situation. You have to strike him as hard as you can, every time, in a target, to smash it beyond functionality.

### 2. Go in 100% dedicated to tearing his head off.

If your intent is anything less than full-bore, you will get less than effective results. If you don't want to hurt him, don't worry, you won't. He may not be so kind to return the favor if given half the chance. You can't afford to screw around—the only way his ribs are going to break is if you make every effort to break them.

This all-or-nothing approach will save your ass—it gets him to nonfunctional so rapidly and efficiently it's over before you know it. This is where you have to take it, as soon as you decide it's on; you have to finish it on your terms, immediately. You cannot afford to get drawn into any back and forth—you need to injure him, take control of the situation and end it on your terms now. Ironically enough, that's the best way to avoid killing someone. You haven't given the situation time to escalate. Sure, you broke his ribs. Broken bones heal. Flesh grows back. If it gets to the point where there's a knife sticking out between someone's ribs, though ... that's another story altogether.

### 3. Go for non-lethal targets.

You probably don't want to start things off with a fist to the throat. Or a stick to the head. Or a knife through the solar plexus. In general, you're going to want to stay away from targets and striking profiles you know to be lethal. And together with that, be sure to use tool configurations that change the nature of the injury (an open hand to the throat instead of a forearm; a forearm to the side of the neck instead of a knee drop).

But let's be brutally honest here—don't be fooled into thinking this changes anything, really. Anytime you enter into a physically violent situation, there's the possibility of someone dying. The best you can do is limit those chances by not doing anything you know for a fact will kill him.

### 4. *Understand that once you go physical with him, his take on what's at stake may change dramatically.*

Perhaps he was only thinking of 'teaching you a lesson,' but now he's afraid for his life and willing to defend it with lethal force (pulling a tool or otherwise 'getting serious'). If you're going in with less than everything you've got, chances are you'll screw up, lose control of him and give him an opportunity to, for argument's sake, shoot you dead. Also, be aware that he may have allies who may come to his aid—be fully prepared to have to injure pretty much everyone in his vicinity. Don't assume you know who his friends are. The same guys who found him an embarrassment when he was spouting nonsense might be willing to kick your butt for laying a hand on him.

Those last two issues—the fact that he could die regardless of how 'careful' you are and the fact that your crossing into the physical plane can get you killed—are the chief reasons I don't recommend using violence as a tool in antisocial interaction. More often than not, your life (losing it or changing it forever) just isn't worth whatever it is you're 'fighting' for. Betting your life in order to win it back will always make sense—that is, in essence, what the asocial is all about.

The above issues are what you need to be aware of, in advance, should you decide to use the tool of violence in an antisocial situation. Whether the situation has turned or spiraled out of 'social tool' control or other factors lead you to act, you need to know what you're getting yourself into and enter into that decision with full knowledge of the pitfalls and possible outcomes. While I will never expressly recommend it, sometimes you are forced into a position where it's either that, or take a beating (or worse) that risks your own well-being.

What I will recommend is being smart about such things and hewing always to the idea of exhausting all options when given the luxury of a choice, and carving a path of destruction through him when you're not.

## Mechanics of the Sucker Punch

*Disclaimer  -  There are serious legal and moral problems with injuring someone who isn't trying to injure you or hasn't otherwise threatened you with serious harm or death.   For the sake of this discussion on the idea of the sucker punch, or otherwise taking people out from behind or when they don't know it's coming, we're going to assume you are right to do it—that your impression of the situation is such that you believe inaction on your part will get you (and/or others) seriously injured or killed.*

To injure or not to injure?

We all know what to do when someone comes after us—get in there and cause an injury, then repeat until satisfied. But what if the man hasn't 'crossed the line' physically, but has let it be known to you, overtly or not, that violence is in the offing? This is everything from a terrorist telling you to sit back down on an airplane to a mugger making his demand, "Give me your wallet," and all the way down to a simple, "You're not leaving here," as you try to go out the door after a party.

You may stand there a split second, taken slightly aback by the seemingly social interaction—he spoke to you with arms crossed, rather than hitting you, or even cocking back to hit you, or even laying hands on you at all.

Now what?

This is where the judgment call starts. If you decide to work it out with social tools, then go for it. I wouldn't recommend it with the terrorist (as we now know all too well), the mugger could go either way depending on your personal read of the situation, and the jerk at the party is even less clear cut.

If you want to go physical and start injuring him, it's best to dive in and get it done as soon as you make the decision. Waiting around to see how it develops gives the man more traction, control, and confidence over the situation—this is how one man with a blade can take over an entire room full of people. The longer it goes on, the more in charge he is. If you take him as soon as you realize it's a bad situation, he never gets the opportunity to assert social dominance. For any kind of hostage-taker, the most critical portion is first contact with the potential hostages. This is where he'll either get everyone to capitulate, or it'll all go to hell for him. It's your job to punch his ticket and get him to tell Charon you said 'hi.'

Let's backtrack a little and take a look at the realities of violent conflict for the average law-abiding taxpayer.

In all reality, you're probably going to be the one getting sucker punched. Because you're not out looking for it, on the hunt, prowling for victims, you'll typically know it's on because someone is trying to do it to you first. Your part in this is easy—if you can still think and move, you'll crush his testicles or gouge his eye (or maybe some of both). Anecdotally, this is how it goes—"There I was, minding my own business, when this guy comes out of nowhere and punches me in the head." The next part of the story is about looking at a target and wrecking it. "So I look up from the ground and see his knee as he's stepping in and I rolled into him and broke it." The rest of the story you know. Or at least can guess. (I'll give you a hint: the guy survived to tell his version of the story).

This is how it will probably come to you. Out of the blue, when you're sick or tired, or otherwise encumbered. When you least expect it. Almost by definition.

When you're walking around with your head up, bristling with vigor, you send an unconscious message. When you walk like you know how to break a leg, predators read it and go looking for the stragglers in the herd.

So most of the time you're avoiding bad situations by simply looking like you know what you're doing. I'm not talking about being a 'badass' or walking around like you've got an attitude—everyone can see right through that (except maybe white suburban kids). If you go to a truly rough part of town the scary ones aren't the jumpy, theatrically hardcore types. They're putting on an act the same way many prey animals try to look like predators in nature (there's a kind of caterpillar that has eyes on its butt so it looks like a small snake, for example). No, the scariest people are the calm, quiet ones. Why are they so damn calm? Because they know they're the apex predators. Nothing hunts them, so why worry?

So what about that weird middle ground—the halfway point between getting sucker punched and the complete wave-off? We're back at the party and the guy at the door crosses his arms and simply says, "You're not leaving." If you choose violence at this point, is there a 'best way' to get into it?

As detailed above, the best way is now. You can throw out all pretense and concepts of technique and simply go for your target. Any defensive moves on his part are moot as long as you don't play that game—if you're going to compete with him, tit-for-tat, strike for block, then, yeah, he stands a chance. If you just wade in to beat him broken, that's what will happen.

This is why I try to get everyone off the idea of waiting, looking, and blocking. It's a sucker's game. For every two you block, the third one'll get you. Out of all the video footage of violence I've seen, none of it—exactly zero—had anyone 'defending themselves' successfully. The successful party was always—every single time—the one who did the beating. Or stabbing. Or whatever. The one doing it got it done. The one trying to stop it got done. Period.

So, if you're worried about what he'll do, you're already on the wrong track. Instead of worrying about what he's going to do, make him do something. Like lie down and hug his shattered knee.

That's not to say there aren't some interesting tactical considerations to take in executing an initial strike—there are, and we'll be looking at them in detail, below—it's just that they are minor and completely subordinate to the idea of wading in and causing injury, first and foremost. Don't get caught in the trap of 'fancy.' Stick with what works because it works. Even if it seems 'beneath you' in its simplicity.

### 1. How to strike when he's not looking.

Alright, this one's obvious. Just pick a target and wreck it. But everyone here already knew that.

### 2. How to strike when he is looking.

We're back at the party. The man is standing between you and the door, thick arms crossed over his barrel chest. He just told you you're not leaving and now he's staring right at you, daring you to defy him. We'll assume that other details of the scenario have led you to believe you are in danger (that's why you were leaving, after all) and you want to get through him and out the door now.

There are two limitations of human vision you can exploit. The first is the fact that when you look straight ahead while standing, you can't see your own feet. This blind spot is created by the lower part of your face, especially the cheekbones. So he can't see anything that comes up inside a 45° angle off his cheekbones. This is why uppercuts work so well. Any low body shot will work, as well as strikes to the groin using hands/arms or knee/shin.

If he's looking you in the eye, he won't see the boot to the groin until it's too late. And here's where we get into some advanced targeting because if you look down at his groin before you strike him, you'll tip him off. Your targeting needs to be good enough that you know how to triangulate your foot into his groin based on where you can see his head is. (This ability grows from lots and lots of floor time with another human body, striking targets in all kinds of orientations).

The second limitation of human vision has to do with the fact that we are all predators. There are specific receptors in your eyes to detect motion across a static background. There's wetware in your head that is specifically wired into these receptors to gage rate of travel and predict where the motion is going.

What this means is that if you throw a big roundhouse motion, like a John Wayne-style haymaker or other large overhand motion that breaks your silhouette and travels across the static background behind you, every human being on the planet is hardwired to see it, clock it, and intercept it. In the old days it would be to hit a bird with a stick. Today it could be for him to simply get his hands up over his face and muck up your strike.

(As a side note, this is one reason people get killed by trains. It is incredibly difficult for us to judge the speed something is going when it's coming dead-on. Laterally, across a static background, and we peg it. Coming straight at us, we're not so good at. Folks walking on the tracks routinely misjudge the amount of time they have until the train is upon them—and the error typically kills them.)

So if he's looking at you, don't break your silhouette—use straight moves that go into the target from inside your outline. Stepping in and driving your fist into his solar plexus (with your elbow in nice and tight at your hip) fills the bill.

As an example of manipulating both limitations, look at a claw to the eyes. It should come up from underneath his vision and inside your silhouette, not from the far outside like an open hand slap.

- And just to reiterate the Important Stuff:
- It doesn't matter if he knows it's coming or not—get him.
- Trying to play this stuff like chess at 90 mph will get you hit by the freight train of violence and send game pieces flying everywhere.

- It's not a game, so don't try to 'play' it.
- Injure him now.

## Manipulating Social Conventions

This is even more morally problematic, as we are now delving into the use of social tools to maneuver people into position for asocial opportunity. This is what the top-end, most cunning sociopaths are very, very good at—like the American mass-murderer Ted Bundy, for example. Everyone who met him said he was singularly charming; he typically used contrived social devices to lure victims into range (wearing a fake cast on his arm, or walking on crutches).

This may be morally rough ground we're on at this point, but the misuse of social tools is brutally effective.

The most basic use would be the 'false capitulation.' This is where you pretend to give up to get an opportunity to injure him. It can be everything from talking to him, "It's cool," or "Okay, you got me, I give up," to simple body language, palms up, arms spread. Or a combination of the two to get you in close enough to strike while getting him to lower his Defcon level. I know people who have done this, and it works great.

You can also talk to him to get him to look away. Ask a question and point, and as he looks, drop him. It's a popular tactic of muggers to approach their victim and ask what time it is. When they look down at their watch, the mugger strikes, having manipulated the situation to regain surprise.

A more advanced, and insidious, version is using your social tools to befriend him. Get him to close distance to shake hands. Then break him.

Of course the big question in everyone's mind right now is, "how can I keep from getting taken by these tricks?" The big one is to trust your gut—people trying to hide something look like they have something to hide. This may manifest itself as small, consciously undetectable 'tells' that you will pick up unconsciously. Your unconscious will then attempt to communicate with you by giving you a 'gut reaction.' Queasiness, butterflies, or other uneasiness. Trust your gut and act on it. Ask questions later.

To wrap up, there are some interesting tactical considerations you can exploit when going in first—when the situation is teetering on the razor's edge between social and full-blown asocial. You can exploit the limitations human vision to 'hide' a strike and you can use social tools to manipulate people to your advantage—getting them to move, look away, or disregard you as a threat.

But all of these things pale in comparison to wading in now and injuring him. If he knows it's coming and can see it's coming that awareness will only work in his favor if you're playing by rules—if you are in competition mode. Then it will be a tit-for-tat exchange. If you wade in simply to beat him toothless and unconscious, then that's what's going to happen—whether he saw it coming, or not.

# Chapter Eleven

## The Absence of Choice

**Violence starts where choice ends.**

For social and antisocial interactions, this means you get to choose whether or not to be involved, and how deep your involvement will go. On the asocial side, you won't have that choice.

This gives us a nice, clean delineator between violence and Everything Else. As you've heard me say time and time again: if you have to ask, the answer is probably 'no.' The reason I say that is because once you commit, your choices dwindle dramatically. Once you cross that line, you're in it 'til you finish it. There are, to be sure, small choices to make—which target to wreck next, when to stop—but none of them involve 'unviolencing' him. Once you break that wrist, you can never go back to just holding hands.

**Make the choice you can live with.**

Be man enough to be called a coward. I've walked away from situations where I was legally and morally in the right and no one present would have objected if I'd laid the jerk out. I've walked away while dodging ego-withering epithets and slurs to the accompaniment of the loud and obvious sound of my social standing peg being taken down a notch. I did this gladly because I was handed the luxury of choice and, to be quite frank, I just didn't feel like it. 'It' being the stomping, the screaming, and then having to do it to all his friends while getting punched in the head three or four times, maybe getting stabbed or shot or killed, or arrested and spending the night in jail, making bail, paying a lawyer and then getting sued. Not to mention having to look over my shoulder every time I stop to take a piss. All that crap is worth my life, but it's not worth my time.

Social standing is a manufactured illusion; losing it is nothing compared to the loss of an eye, or freedom, or your life. If your friends are truly your friends they will remain so; everyone else can go hang.

Asocial means you have no choice; or rather, the choice is something decidedly unchoosy like 'kill or be killed.' (Which one would you pick? Yeah, everybody picks that one, too). Because it's hallmarked by a lack of communication, asocial comes on without warning, without preamble, like lightning out of a clear blue sky. One minute you're worried about which curry joint to patronize and the next you're getting stabbed. You're down to those small choices, like which target to wreck next, and when to stop.

Once you're out of choices, you have one choice left: give it your all or play games. If you choose the latter, you've handed all the power of choice to the other guy. From a purely mechanical point of view, in social and antisocial situations he gets to choose whether or not a technique works. All of your sundry come-alongs, pain compliance, joint locks and submission holds fall into this category. If he decides you 'got him' and gives up, all well and good. If he decides the pain in his wrist doesn't matter, well, now you're stuck holding the tiger by the tail. And your Plan B better be really, really sharp. Especially if the choice he makes is to take it into the asocial and get to the work of injuring you.

For some people, the difference between antisocial and asocial is really problematic. They're the ones who interpret every sideways look as a challenge to fight. For you, on the other hand, it's really simple. Just remember that:

### 1. *You don't have to worry about saving your pride.*

You know what you're capable of, and beating someone up (or breaking his ribs) isn't going to change that. And if your friends are people who lose respect for you because you choose not to start breaking heads, well, you might want to take another look at y our friends. That's where you do have a choice!

**2. *Antisocial interactions can seem asocial, and they can become asocial.***

But like I keep saying, until there is absolutely no chance of walking away, you're still in the antisocial arena. You, and often you alone, have the power to defuse this bomb and make sure no one gets hurt. Or, you could choose to take things into the asocial arena. Just hope you're not dealing with someone who's going to hunt you down and pay you back in kind—or worse.

**3. *The moment you stop thinking "Should I hit this guy?" and start swinging, that's when you've stepped into the realm of violence.***

If you're asking if you should, you shouldn't. Period.

## When No Choice Matters

Fortunately for you, once you enter that asocial sphere, you're not the only one who loses the luxury of choice. For both you and him, this has become a kill-or-be-killed event. You're both in there hardcore, giving it your all, and your single goal is to give it to him first and hard. Why? Because if you want to be the one walking away, you have to remove all aspect of choice from his life—at least for the time being.

The mechanics of the asocial, violent, interaction can be summed up in a single word: injury. Injury removes choice from the equation. He has no say in whether or not his eye comes out of his skull or if his throat crushes. He has no say in how his body will move next. The physical laws of the universe, and how well you've employed them, are the only arbiters here. If you did it right, everything breaks. He may wish double-plus hard on a falling star it wasn't so, but it's not going to matter one whit. Violence is the absence of choice, and he's just along for the ride.

# PART TWO:

# THE PRINCIPLES
# OF VIOLENCE

# Chapter One

## Fight or Flight

*"No passion so effectually robs the mind of all its powers of acting and reasoning as fear."*  —Edmund Burke

People often ask me about the "fight-or-flight" response when it comes to responding to a violent, imminent threat of physical attack. When I tell them that there are actually four responses to this type of threat I usually get a confused looked.

As a lifelong student of violence I constantly research sources from the academic and literary world that deal with this very controversial subject. Some of my research has led me to see fight-or-flight as a fallacy. Fight-or-flight is a viable response, but only when the threat occurs between two different species. If you are walking through the woods and a Kodiak bear starts to rush you, you would quickly either fight if you had a weapon or run (flight) if you did not. Yes, you can use the other two responses but for the most part the meeting of two different species results in fight-or-flight.

So what are the other two responses? What sets a violent human-to-human encounter apart from a violent interspecies encounter?

### The Four Horsemen of Response

When two members of the same species meet with one side posing an imminent threat, the other can respond as follows:

1.  *Fight - The challenge is assessed and the target decides to fight back.*

2.  *Flight - The challenge is assessed and the target decides to evade the threat, or run.*

3. ***Posture - The challenge is assessed and the target decides to feign or posture aggressively with the ultimate goal being to avoid having to fight or flee.***

4. ***Capitulate - The challenge is assessed and the target decides to freeze, lie down, and hope that by submitting s/he will appease the aggressor.***

Most are familiar with the first two options, but let's explore the latter two. How many times have you seen a person issue a threat and move towards someone aggressively, only for the person to respond by yelling back and striking an aggressive, threatening stance? This is very common in social violent situations where there is much posturing for dominance. Often the real objective is to get one side to back down, with verbal threats and aggressive postures used to convey dominance. That is a classic example of the Posture Response.

This is a dangerous gambit for both participants because it delays the fight option and often wastes valuable opportunities to end the situation with the Fight Response. The next response to explore is the all too common Capitulate Response. This is where an aggressive threat is met with complete and immediate submission to the threatening party. This response is very dangerous when used to avoid getting harmed because it literally puts you at the mercy of an aggressor. You rely on their moral code to respect your capitulation and have that be a sufficient way to satiate their desire to aggressively dominate you. Very risky.

However, when used properly the Capitulate Response can be an extremely effective manner to get your aggressor into a vulnerable position to execute the Fight Response. Basically, you're getting the aggressor to expose vulnerable areas of his body to attack by your feigned capitulation.

Why is this important? There are three reasons. First of all, understanding how to use capitulation as a fighting tactic can be extremely useful. But more importantly, you can't enter a violent situation expecting your fear to drive you away. Moreover, it's essential that you not rely on "fight or flight" as an excuse to avoid learning what you need to know in order to defend yourself. Fear is a powerful human emotion, but with practice it won't control you. That's what will really matter in a violent situation.

## Acting in the Face of Fear

For too long fallacies have held sway while common criminals exploit fear and ignorance; the simple facts that govern the effective use of violence as a survival tool are well known to them, and denied to the law-abiding, successfully socialized citizen. Know, then, these simple facts and let your power increase:

### 1. *You can take decisive action in the face of fear.*

The first reaction in any violent situation is that most primal emotion of fear. When a man steps out of the shadows holding a knife, or an intruder pulls open the curtain in your shower, your adrenaline immediately starts pumping and your heart beats faster. These are natural reactions, which cannot be avoided— nor should they be. This is the fight-or-flight survival instinct that allows you to focus completely on destroying your enemy or to get the hell out of there.

Many people fear that they will be overwhelmed by fight-or-flight and behave irrationally or 'freeze up' and be incapable of acting.

When you know how to 'swim in the pool of violence,' however, your reaction will be slightly different. You will still experience the biological fact of fear, but that will be tempered with the knowledge of what to do next. Instead of being shocked and frightened into submission, believing you have no choice but to submit, you'll do what you've trained to do. If that training was to wait and see, or to get ready, you may have already lost.

If, however, that training is for violence—for causing injury—then that's what you'll do.

## 2. *Violence is available to everyone.*

You are a predator born, with stereovision for hunting prey and teeth for ripping and tearing flesh. You are a member of the only species that makes an art of war. The average human body is an awesome engine of destruction, driven by the most dangerous thing in the known universe: a human brain. You are a survival engine, the descendant of winners; your ancestors didn't get you here by laying down and giving up. They made the losers do that. Violence is your birthright.

## 3. *The one doing the violence tends to prevail.*

Violence is one person injuring another person. This is the definition of the effective use of violence. While all violent acts have injury in common, they also share another trait: at the end, the person walking away is typically the one who did it.

## 4. *The one getting the violence done to them tends to get injured.*

Defense wounds are found on corpses. 'Nuff said.

# Chapter Two

## Violence is About Injury

*"It is by no means self-evident that human beings are most real when most violently excited; violent physical passions do not in themselves differentiate men from each other, but rather tend to reduce them to the same state." —Thomas Elliot*

All acts of violence come down to the same thing: injury. By now, you should be ready for that message. Until you accept this basic fact, you'll never be able to defend yourself effectively.

In violent conflict, always assume that your life is on the line. While you can predict how he will react physically to being struck, how he reacts psychologically will vary from individual to individual. Some people may panic and run; others may choose to kill you for daring to defy them. This means you have to be merciless, vicious and methodical. You're going to kick him when he's down. You're going to break his arm, then use it to throw him. And no matter what, you're not going to stop until you're done.

After you land your first blow, assume that he is prepared to go all the way. You might be wrong, but it's better to assume the other man is in it to kill you than to assume he's not and leave your family to mourn your mistake.

This may make violence seem kind of useless in your everyday life. If you're living right, it is. Violence is a very narrow tool; it's only good for one thing, and that's shutting off a human being. It's not really good for anything else. If you're going to pull it out and use it, then employ it to full effect. 'Going easy' on someone who wants to murder you or otherwise screwing around in violent conflict can get you killed.

Every technique and every target is must be exploited, even those you might normally regard as 'out of bounds.' If, for example, you consider eye gouging to be beyond the pale and your only target is his eye, your hesitation could cost you your life. (Employing violence to it's fullest has an added benefit. Remember that people flock to a social fight and flee from actual violence. When you get in and break him with brutal efficiency, stomping him when he's down and whatnot, anyone not involved, like innocent bystanders, will take off running. Anyone you need to pay attention to will make themselves known by closing distance and coming after you. Put one man down and you'll find out who his accomplices are.)

### The Injury Manifesto

There is a single key feature that is present in every successful use of violence: injury. It defines the act and brands the participants, the vanquished more so than the victor. Owning injury, the arbiter of success in violence, gives you a distinct advantage over those whose understanding is dim and instinctual. Know, then, these simple facts and let your power increase.

### Violence Begins and Ends with Injury

Violence is purely about injury. Injury is the only thing that means anything in violence. It's the goal and end-result. It defines the violent act and finishes it. Violence literally starts and ends with injury.

Effective violence is hallmarked by serial injury: injuring him, taking advantage of that injury to do it again, and again to put him down, with ever-increasing severity (stomping on a man who's down is easy for you and devastating for him).

### Injury Changes Everything in Your Favor

In violent conflict, injury is the portal through which you pass into the rest of your life. As things go bad—he pulls the gun—your options narrow to a single question: 'action or passivity?' In a way, you are at the end of your life: if he shoots you dead, it's over. The thumb in the eye, however, is the key turning in the lock on the rest of your days. Injury gives you options; a universe of choices spreads before you. Injury is opportunity.

## Injury is Objective

Disinterested third parties can all agree that an injury has occurred. A broken leg is obvious from across the street.

## Injury Decrements Body Function

It will alter the normal functioning of his body in a negative way. A broken leg just plain doesn't work.

## Injury is Permanent

That is, it's permanent across the course of the encounter. It will require medical attention in order to heal. A broken leg does not get better on it's own. He can't 'walk it off.'

## Injury is Physics and Physiology Meeting Badly

Excessive force plus vulnerable anatomical target equals injury. There is nothing in this equation about pain or the psychological state of the recipient. Neither of these matters. Different people have different pain thresholds; for some, a torn fingernail drops them into dramatic paroxysms of agony, for others a torn off limb goes unnoticed. But note that in the case of the missing limb, that person may be functioning just fine psychologically, but they're not going to be grabbing and picking anything up anytime soon.

## Injury is Independent of Technique

All we need is force and a target. You could trip and fall, all by yourself, and get an injury. Note the conspicuous lack of a hopped-up emotional state, a technique, or even another person. This fact is why technique without injury is a parlor trick, and injury, regardless of how it occurred (with technique or without, 'accidentally,' etc.) will always be more effective.

The most artless injury will always be superior to the fanciest technique. Rock to the head, anyone?

## All Injuries are Equal

This is another way of saying all targets are equal. The best target? The one you just wrecked. All injuries are equal when you know what to do next—how to take advantage of the fact you injured him.

## Injured People Move in Predictable Ways

The body responds to injury through the somatic reflex arc (spinal reflexes). These are pre-programmed, specific movements, triggered by a large stimulus (like ruptured testicles). The threshold switch that decides whether or not to reflex is in the spinal cord, not the brain. There is no conscious choice involved. Just physics and physiology. These reflexes are injury-specific, meaning that a boot to the groin elicits the same basic response in all humans.

This means you can predict how he'll move when you injure him—and be there to take full advantage of it.

## Injured People are Helpless

For the short moment of time they are in the throes of their spinal reflex, they cannot stop you from injuring them again. And again. And again...

## Injury Begets Injury

An adjunct to the helplessness above, as beating an injured man is easy work. It's also shorthand for 'a broken knee can cause head trauma.'

## Injury Trumps Speed, Strength and Resolve

Is he stronger than you? Not with a crushed throat he isn't. Is he faster than you? Not with a broken knee. Is he far more dangerous than you, with scads of training, experience, a gun, and an indomitable iron will? Funny how a broken neck takes all the scary out of him.

## Violence Begins and Ends with Injury

Anything you do in a violent situation that does not cause an injury is worthless to you. Every time you touch him, you need to break something inside him. Every time you touch him, you need to make a part of him cease normal function. Injure him, drop him, and keep on injuring him until he's nonfunctional. You're not done until you're sure he's done.

The answer to every question in violent conflict is: injury, now.

## What is Injury Really?

It's the only thing that means anything in violence, or at least that's what we're always saying. But what is injury after all? And is there a simpler way to think of it, relate to it and thereby better relate it to others? We'll start with the dictionary definition of the word—The Shorter OED, 5th Ed. says:

*'Hurt or loss caused to or sustained by a person or thing; harm, detriment; damage, esp. to the body; an instance of this.'*

This is a good start, but it's not quite as serious and stunning as I would like. While 'harm, detriment, damage' are all good synonyms for what we're up to, it's still a little bit vague on the overall effect we're gunning for. There are plenty of people out there, for example, who believe that they can sustain 'damage' and keep going. And, of course, they're right. We all can. But no one—NO ONE—can sustain injury the way we mean it and keep going. Period. So even the dictionary leaves something to be desired, a 'tightening up' of ambiguities.

These ambiguities flourish and grow into their own chaos-gardens in the minds of the average person. I dare say no two people's definition of 'injury' is going to be exactly the same. For some it is tearing a fingernail or stubbing a toe; others won't declare it until blood is spilled. The difference between the definitions of a lucky person unused to pain and a trauma surgeon is going to be vast. It's a lot like saying the word 'dog' out loud to a roomful of people: everyone will see a dog in their mind's eye, but I dare say no two will be alike.

And still, for me, even with torn skin and spilled blood, we are not at a workable definition.

The TFT 'textbook' definition reads thusly:

*'The disruption of human tissue in a specific anatomical feature such that normal function is obviously impaired (and can only be regained through medical intervention), eliciting an involuntary spinal reflex reaction.'*

This is great for two reasons: it reinforces the universality of violence (as this effect can be achieved with any judicious application of kinetic energy, from fist to stick to bullet) as well as being specific enough to rule out hangnails and messy, but ultimately ineffective, minor lacerations.

The only problem is that for all its precise 'lawyer-ese' it's quite a mouth—and mind—ful. It's not easy to remember, it doesn't roll of the tongue, and you're just plain not going to win over any converts with it. It's thorough but clunky. By seeking to be clear it loses its clarity and becomes next to worthless to you. Anything that gets in the way of your understanding needs to be retooled—like carving steps into an insurmountable cliff face.

This gets us to my current favorite way to think of injury:

Break things inside of people so they don't work anymore.

This is the way the sociopath approaches the problem, the way the Saturday night slugger thinks when he wades in to deliver a beat-down. It is the simplest way to think of injury. It paints a picture that's easy to parse; even the ambiguities work in your favor. Does 'they' refer to the people or the things inside them? Hey, either one or both: I'm good with all of it.

This is a definition of injury you can take as your personal violence mission statement. It's all you want to do; it's the only measuring stick that divides success from failure. Easy to think, easy to say, easy to do.

# Chapter Three

## Why You Must Learn to Kill

*"It is better to die on your feet than to live on your knees!"*
—*Emiliano Zapata*

If you were uncomfortable with the last chapter, you're not going to like this one very much. It contains some things that are hard to take but have to be said. I won't sugarcoat it: you must go into every violent situation with the intent to cause serious injury and, if necessary, death. The time has come to point out a harsh truth: the biggest fear most people have is realizing they actually can be every bit as brutal—and effective—as the most heinous thug walking the street.

The obvious difference between a slap-fight and a murder is one of intent. You have to have that intent. You have to go in willing to injure and even kill the person who's trying to kill you. But unless you have scary psychic powers or you really can throw daggers with your eyes, intent, in and of itself, is not what's going to get the job done. So what is intent really doing? What lies between intent and injury?

Body weight in motion

When one has intent, they apply themselves totally to causing injury. A total dedication of will tends to manifest itself as a total dedication of body mass. There is no hesitation, no getting ready, no waiting to see what will happen next. There is only rapid, brutal motion. The knife punched through ribs, again and again.

But I Don't Want to Become the Bad Guy!

When confronted with the realities of violence, sane, well-socialized people recoil. Violence is the void oblivion in which nothing save injury exists; it is a hellish monospace where things like communication, love, and caring are not just absent, they never were.

It is a space defined by the absence of all we hold dear.

It is Nietzsche's Abyss.

It is natural, and indeed 'good' in a social sense, for the mind to recoil from such a thing. But then a secondary reaction occurs; the mind recoils and then seeks, desperately, to fill in the gap between itself and that awful space. To build a wall of easy ideas in order to maintain a sanity-safe distance. You can hit a guy in the head with a rock, or you can do a back flip and then hit him in the head with a rock. Either way, he gets a head trauma. Remember, Occam's Razor says: "Forget fancy—the tire-iron to the head trumps all."

This Guy's a Killer

During my time in Las Vegas, I met a number of Mixed Martial Arts competitors from various "No-Holds-Barred" events like the UFC and Pride. For the most part, these fighters were amazing physical specimens and tremendous competitors. Their skills in the arena were impressive and fun to watch. And surprisingly, the fighters I met were all very good-natured guys.

At one event I was introduced by an MMA friend of mine to one of the top competitors, and this fighter asked, through his interpreter, if I was an MMA competitor.

Before I could answer, my friend (who had a couple of beers in him since he was not on this fight card) smiled and said, "Nah, Tim's a 'killer.' He likes to teach you how to stab people to death or beat their brains out with a tire iron. You'd like his course!"

(It's always great to have friends give this kinda PR "help").

Then the fighter asked if I taught how to "defend" against knives and guns. Again, my friend "answered" for me saying "Oh yeah, and more than one attacker, too. I mean, its prison riot training!"

(Again, very "helpful" stuff. By now, I'm sure the interpreter's really wondering about me!)

Then the fighter told of his cousin being assaulted and stabbed by two men in his home country. He said he felt bad because he truly couldn't give his cousin (who survived the attack) any tips on how to "fight" people with knives.

"Quite frankly, for all my skills in the ring, I doubt I could have done much better. I know how to kick someone's ass on the mat but on the street, it's so different."

We exchanged info and he got the dates when I'd be training in Europe that year. Then he was off to prepare for his match (which he easily won that night, absolutely wrecking his opponent).

But his words got me thinking about the difference between a fighter and a "killer:"

- The fighter competes to better his opponent; the "killer" focuses solely on ending the other person.

- The fighter seeks to score points or force a submission; the "killer" seeks to shut down the other's brain.

- The fighter is good at kicking someone's ass; the "killer" knows how to irreparably injure vulnerable areas of the human body, permanently wrecking the functioning of that area.

- The fighter relies on superior strength, speed and skill; the "killer" gets his results using stealth and the action of violence.

- The fighter's skills work best in the controlled environment of the ring; the "killer" is effective anywhere violence is necessary.

- The fighter's skills deteriorate once his competitive years end; the "killer" retains his skills often for a lifetime.

I could go on, but you see the pattern.

Here's the point: you must always ask yourself, "How will I apply my martial arts or combat sport training?" 'Cause if it's in the random chaos found in the world of real violence then you hamstring yourself with rules and skills that work mainly for the young, fast, and strong.

And we're not even addressing whether the other guy plays by your rules (wanna guess how much time most murderers spend worrying about your competitive standards?).

That's why I challenge you to explore the world of the "killer" (even if you're pursuing a competitive MMA career). Despite your likely repulsion at the term, these skills are easily learned and can last your entire lifetime. But most important is the by-product of learning this—you get to live a far more relaxed and peaceful life.

Strange, I realize, but true.

Finally, understand the big difference between a "killer" and a murderer.

Face-to-face with the later, it's the skill set of the "killer" that not only prepares you to survive. It can actually give you the advantage.

## Lethal Force

No cop wants to draw his gun, but if some psychopath comes running at him with a knife, you better believe he'll do it. When it's your life or his, you have to be ready to make a choice. Is your moral stance against killing strong enough that you'll let some sociopathic murderer end your life for no reason? If the answer is no, you'd better be prepared to use lethal force when you have to.

You need the skills to kill, and if it's clear that it's life or death, then killing is in order. The severity of the situation can be surmised in many different ways (hostage situation in which other hostages are being killed right in front of you, modern airline hijack, firearms, and associated threats of imminent death, etc.), but ultimately it's going to come down to a personal call on your part. And your best guideline is to trust your gut.

If you don't think it's a particularly bad situation you're probably picking up unconscious cues from body language, facial expressions, etc., that are telling you he's not serious. If you feel serious apprehension in your gut—that queasy, 'oh my God' feeling—you're picking up those same unconscious cues but this time they're lethal. He means to kill you, and primitive parts of your brain are trying to let you know by making you feel sick.

For all of that, ultimately it's your call. We can't build every possible scenario you could ever be involved in, and we can't tell you how you should think and feel. It's all up to you; you have to live or die with your decision.

Once you do go in, go in full-bore, to tear his head off. How far you take it will depend on what you need to feel done, safe, and able to turn your back on him and walk away. Every use of violence must start with serious injury, and then proceed to rendering him nonfunctional.

This can mean one or more of three things:

- Incapacitation
- Unconsciousness
- Death

Incapacitation is everything from a single shot to the ribs that drops him and makes him go fetal and quit to a broken knee and two broken collar bones that make it impossible for him to get up. At what point you've reached incapacitation and can stop is your personal judgment call. Just make damn sure you feel comfortable turning your back on him.

Unconsciousness is just that: he's out cold and down for the count. It's obvious when you've achieved it. He'll be down, motionless, possibly with his jaw slack and eyes rolled back in his head. Once you've got this it's safe to say you're done.

Killing the man by stomping on this throat, breaking his neck, or stabbing him in the heart is reserved for the most extreme circumstances only. Situations where you realize or believe that you or others will be killed if you do not act. You need to think a great deal about how you feel about his and make your choices ahead of time: you don't want to get caught hesitating when what's required is decisive action.

# Chapter Four

## Overcoming the Stigma of Violence

*"Violence isn't always evil. What's evil is the infatuation with violence." —Jim Morrison*

Hopefully, by now you've come to realize that I don't endorse using violence for the reasons a criminal sociopath would. I don't think violence should ever be used to get what you want, and I think in all situations, it's a last resort.

But when it becomes your only option, you have to be ready to act.

People are afraid of violence. They're afraid of experiencing it, and they're afraid of being the one to do it. If you go into a room full of people and start talking about gouging eyes, they're going to freak out. We live in a society that's safe on the surface, and no one wants to think about what lies underneath.

But something does lie underneath, and if you ever encounter it, there's only one way to survive it. And in order to do that, you have to accept violence as a tool—not good or evil and of itself, but a tool that can be used for good or evil depending on who gets a hold of it and how they're swinging it.

Violence is a tool, and as such it takes on the moral color of the user—but only after the fact. Bludgeoning someone to death with a claw hammer can be murder in one instance and justified homicide in another—but in both cases someone bludgeoned someone else to death with a claw hammer. Knowing how doesn't make you a bad person. Using that knowledge to bully and intimidate others is a far cry from using that knowledge to protect yourself and your family.

## How Much is "Too Much?"

Most people are willing to accept that violence can come in handy. If you say to someone, "I know self-defense," you'll get a very different reaction than if you say to someone, "I know how to kill people." But the first is an empty, generic term, and in a real life-or-death encounter with asocial violence, it's not going to see you through.

Now, I'm not saying you should go around bragging about knowing how to kill people—that's just stupid. But you should know how to do it, and you shouldn't be ashamed of the fact.

Society would really rather that you meet force with like force; if he just wants to push, you're allowed to push; if he just wants to slap and choke, you're allowed to slap and choke ... and if he wants to kill you, you're allowed to match him in kind. That's great— as long as he doesn't get the 'kill' idea before you do. Of course, if he just wants to slap and you break him, people will call that 'excessive.' I find it hilarious. It shows a basic misunderstanding of violence itself. There's no such thing as 'excessive force' when it comes to hurting people—violence is the art excess.

There are lots of examples floating around of precision knockout blows—restrained force that results in a successful attack or defense. But in pretty much every such video circulating on the Internet, we see the results of a perfect storm: there was just enough penetration and rotation through a target to get the desired outcome. The conditions were sufficient to get an injury, but almost always hardly optimal. The perfect storm usually consists of luck-factors like the injured man moving into the strike (increasing penetration & body weight effects) and/or being caught off-guard and flat-footed.

But what about the times when he's moving away from the strike? Or 'rolls' with the punch? In that case sufficiency fails to result in an injury, and now you can see how this is sub-optimal. Sometimes you get a knockout and sometimes you don't. That's fine and dandy in the ring, but you can't bet your life on such things.

Your job is to figure out what is sufficient to cause the injury, and then optimize it to ensure that you get exactly that set of circumstances every single time.

Penetration and rotation through a target, anyone?

Maximizing penetration means that even if he's moving away or 'rolling' with it he's going to get overrun: you're going to get a good three feet of follow-through through the target—with your entire mass behind it.

Maximizing rotation is you taking full advantage of that three feet you bought yourself with the penetration: you will make the target bounce off of the tool, rather than the other way around.

So with so-called sufficient force, if we get lucky, we catch him with just the right amount of 'snap' at the end of that punch to give him a concussion: so out of ten wild swings we get the one that connects and gets the job done. Again, if we're lucky.

With optimal, we get the knockout (or whatever injury we're gunning for) every single time, and only luck (and unusual circumstance, like you screwing something up) is going to prevent it.

Look at it this way: blowing on some embers you made by rubbing two sticks together in a heap of dried pine needles is sufficient to start a fire, but, as anyone who's earned that merit badge can attest, 'sufficient' doesn't mean 'every time.' It can take all day.

We can optimize our situation by firing a flare gun into a ruptured gasoline tanker truck. Now that's gonna make a big BOOM every single time.

Overdoing it? Yes, and that's the point.

Injury in violence is, by definition, the result of excess. The body only breaks when it is subjected to forces that exceed the elasticity of human tissue.

And while there are those who will tell you that sufficient is 'just enough', that's only good in theory. While it could work every time, in practice it often doesn't. Optimal means it will work every time.

Sufficient hopes for a perfect storm. Optimal recreates that storm, every time, through excess, brutality, and methodical thoroughness.

Call it precision brutality, if you will.

# Chapter Five

## Violence as the Ultimate Survival Tool

*"One should always play fairly when one has the winning cards" —Oscar Wilde*

The reason it's so important to view violence as a tool for survival came to me during a conversation with a friend of mine named Chuck, a former NFL Defensive Lineman. Chuck had a reputation in college as a brawler and never missed an opportunity to use his fists to answer any disagreement.

Chuck has definitely mellowed over the years and is much easier to be around these days—but old habits die hard. The conversation drifted towards my training and he was giving me some feedback from a mutual friend who attended a TFT seminar.

Our friend Tony loved the training and, since he travels to some of the more dangerous parts of the world, has unfortunately had to use his training. The results were that he survived two unavoidable criminal attacks using principles and methods from the TFT Seminar.

Tony faced multiple attackers in one incident and a knife in the other. Chuck was impressed that Tony survived both incidents unscathed and then commented that the three attackers were all larger than Tony, as was the knife wielder, and that in a "fair fight" Tony would have lost.

He pointed out that if Tony hadn't used all that "unfair stuff" he got from my seminar he never would have "won". Chuck said he was glad that Tony knew TFT but that it really didn't prove he could fight.

Chuck went on to say that if it were just a "thumping contest"—"Ya know, Tim, a real fight," then the bigger, stronger guy would always win. He was disturbed by the fact that Tony had to crush the throat of one of his attackers and actually kill the guy who tried to knife him. To Chuck, that proved it wasn't a "real fight." In addition, the fact Tony effectively used deception to disarm his attackers before he attacked really disturbed Chuck.

"That's not fighting, it's just..."

"Violence?" I suggested.

"Yeah, it proves nothing about how good a fighter you are," Chuck blurted out.

I know what Chuck was trying to say and it's sad when I see anyone like him that has never gone beyond using violence to dominate a social situation.

By choosing to use violence in a social situation, guys like Chuck always run the risk of bumping into someone who won't bother fighting a bigger, stronger guy.

They'll just use violence in the only way it should be used... as a survival tool.

## A "Fair Fight" Isn't About Survival

Some of you might agree with Chuck. You might think that, although you understand the necessity for some people to understand TFT's methods, a real fight involves two people pitting their strength against each other. That's fine in terms of competition. Unfortunately, a criminal doesn't think that way. He has absolutely no desire to make sure the fight is "fair"—only to make sure he wins.

People often ask me for the best way to "protect" them in some imagined criminal assault. They want me to respond by giving some perfect technique that handles their particular imagined scenario. They're often disappointed at first when I don't respond the way they want me to. They don't like to hear the truth—that violence is random and thinking only in terms of "techniques" to use against a random act is a good way to get yourself killed.

The problem with practically everyone's approach to dealing with violence is not that they're incapable of learning techniques. It's that they don't understand this way of responding to violence—real asocial, maim, cripple, or "kill you now" violence—is seriously flawed.

That's because when it comes to violence, we (meaning you and me, the productive, law-abiding members of society) live lives of assumed constraints.

We are taught early on by parents, teachers, and our legal system that if we want the benefits of living in a society like ours, then we need to constrain our violent impulses when things don't go our way.

And obviously, this is a very good thing. It's the reason you don't kill the obnoxious jerk that steals your parking place, you wait patiently for the light to turn green at an intersection, and you don't shoot the neighbor's Labrador for digging up your rose garden.

When it comes to the subject of violence, we are controlled by society much like circus elephants are controlled by their handlers. These trainers know the most reliable way to handle an elephant is to "condition" it when it is very young. They put a shackle on the baby elephant's leg with a short chain that is held in the ground by a very long spike. The baby elephant tugs at the chain attempting to break free.

After a short while the elephant breaks the skin around the shackled leg and gives up. But the pain of attempting to break free is never forgotten.

Later on, that same method is used to control the now full-grown elephant, even though the adult beast could pull the spike free with no more effort than you and I use to remove a thumbtack from a corkboard.

And the same approach is taken with all productive members of society regarding the tool of violence.

We are "shackled" at a very young age—first at home, later in ours schools, and finally at our workplaces.

When faced with violence, most of us respond socially. We attempt to communicate with our attacker in hopes of avoiding the use of violence. We may threaten to use this tool but we really don't want to since that shackle is still firmly attached.

The sad part of assumed constraints is that most martial arts, combat sports, and, yes, even most "reality fighting systems" teach you to respond—*while still shackled!*

It doesn't work.

I learned long ago the first order of business is to teach my clients how easy it is to break those assumed constraints when the threat warrants such an approach.

Because the real threat to society is when we run up against some "rogue elephant" that has never been "shackled" and has no problem using violence to get what he wants. And imagine how easy it is to fight someone if they have their leg shackled.

Remember first and foremost—violence is rarely the answer to most situations, but when it is the answer, it's the only answer.

Once you understood that you then must be able to rip off those assumed constraints and free yourself so you can utilize the tool of violence when required. This is not the best way to survive an asocial, violent threat: **it is the only way.**

**A Tool For Survival**

In the end, you don't 'win' in violent conflict—you survive it.

It's not competition; it's destruction. The survivor gets to walk away. The other guy doesn't. And far more often than not, the one who's walking away is the one who was doing the violence.

It's only going to work out in your favor if you get in there and injure him. You have to put him down and keep him there. You have to throw out the rules and combine instinct with intellect.

In these situations survival is the only thing that matters, and the best way to survive violence is to be the one doing the violence.

Knowing how to use violence as a survival tool—and being willing to do so—puts you on nice, flat terrain, even and equal with the worst of humanity. You can see the people who still have their heads in the sand and the predators who stalk among them taking advantage. Before you know how to grab the tool of violence in both fists and swing it hard and sure you are at a disadvantage. But learning how to use violence as a survival tool means that disadvantage is gone, and in its place is the stone-cold truth: you're responsible for you, all alone. Either you can rely on yourself or you can't; either you'll get the job done or you won't.

You have a choice: you can be afraid, or you can be resolved.

## The Golden Rule Of Violence: Injure Him Now

The best way to survive violent conflict is to be the first one to cause an injury. When you destroy a target and make him react, you will have the time and the opportunity to injure him again and again and again. You will be in control of the situation, and of the other man. Do unto others before they do unto you!

All of this flies in the face of a "fair fight." But survival situations aren't a fair fight. In a competitive fair fight, it's all about skill and ability. A violent situation is about survival: injure the other guy as fast and hard as you can, in any way possible. It's not something to be used lightly, but when it's the only alternative, it will save your life.

You have to ditch the social constraints and shackles before you're in the situation. It's time to accept that, while these constraints are useful in 99% of everyday situations, you may one day find yourself facing a situation where they don't apply. And in that situation, you have to be able to slip them off and unleash the killer within.

# Chapter Six

## Kill It Simple, Stupid

**Violence is simple.**

How simple is it? We can answer that with two more questions:

*1. How can untrained people prevail?*

*2. How is it that untrained people can prevail over trained people?*

Because for all their blissful naïveté the victorious untrained have a firm grip on the tool of violence. This fact stands because violence is much simpler than people would have you believe; it's much simpler than you want to believe.

The idea that violence is difficult and requires years of training—and that years of training will protect you from the untrained—are comfortable, comforting thoughts. They are society's buffer. Even if you yourself aren't one of the trained, it provides comfort to know that unless someone's had years of training, they aren't really going to be able to damage you. Sit back and relax. Doesn't that feel nice?

I read somewhere once that the little lies we tell ourselves on a daily basis, the small untruths that shape our subjective realities, are what keep us happy. That the people who see the world and themselves as it all 'really is' are the clinically depressed.

Accepting the simplicity of violence is an unpalatable dose of hard reality. To learn that you are never immune and that someone who is completely and conspicuously untrained can murder you is acutely unsettling. Even depressing.

If, that is, you're a blood-bucket-is-half-empty kind of person.

I like to look at it from the other side—the blood bucket is half full, and I'm going to use him to fill it the rest of the way up. If violence is so simple that even the untrained can use it and survive, then even a little bit of training is going to make you really, really good at it.

With a little bit of training you could know far more about wrecking people than a serial killer does. The only thing that could possibly hold you back is a lack of intent; what the serial killer lacks in technique he more than makes up for with a monomaniacal will to get the job done. But you already knew that.

**Violence is much simpler, even, than I present it to be.**

I spent a lot of time teasing out the common elements of violence and finding ways to communicate them to you. It comes across as a ton of material that people mistakenly believe they must master before they can be effective. Let's be honest: I have a lot to say. This stuff is interesting to me, and if you've read this far, I'm guessing it's interesting to you, too. I like to talk about it—to break down those social walls that pretend this stuff doesn't exist. But for all that, we're only ever really talking about the rock to the head ... and what is the rock to the head but a big hunk of kinetic energy driven through a vulnerable target?

Everything else is just detail work, an exploration of all possible combinations and configurations for using your body as a human tissue wrecking machine, with and without snap-on tools. Violence only seems complicated if you buy into the hype, if you think that because someone's falling-down drunk, they can't hurt you, if you think you need a black belt before you can seriously injure someone.

Let's look at it this way: close your eyes and think of the most stunning martial arts action movie sequence you've ever seen. Come on, I know you've seen them—they're everywhere, and they make violence as intricate and beautiful as some sort of dance. Now think about the end result of that complex series of leaps, jumps, throws, and movements. It was a guy down on the ground, dead or injured, right?

So in other words, that beautiful build-up is exactly that: a build-up. It has absolutely nothing to do with causing actual, physical injuries. It looks impressive. If you shout a lot, it sounds impressive. And if you're dealing with a normal person, it might be enough to scare them into backing down, hesitating, or making a bad mistake.

But we've all seen the flip side, too: the moment in an action movie where some guy comes up twisting, turning, hopping, flipping, and doing every martial arts move known to man ... until our hero punches him in the face, and down he goes. That's a slightly more realistic assessment of how violence works. When you focus your energy on techniques, execution, and style, that means you're not focusing on what violence is really about: hurting people.

Remember, in a life-or-death situation, technique won't save your life. Hops and yells, throws and flips, none of it matters. When the chips are down, every single movement should be directed at a single cause: injury.

So forget everything you think you know about how it should go down: violence is you injuring people. It's throwing yourself at him to break things inside of him. You are the bull in his anatomical china shop, the Enola Gay to his Hiroshima. It's you violating every tenet of polite society and destroying the only thing that any of us ever really own. And if that violates your personal philosophy, counters your techniques, or seems unsporting, then you haven't really listened to a word I've said. Because violence is never about competition. It's not about showing off or practicing your coolest moves. Save that stuff for the arena. When we start talking about life-or-death violence, your whole focus has to be on survival—and in this case, survival means causing more damage to him than he does to you.

It's simpler than you think because it has nothing to do with thinking. Violence is all in the doing.

# Chapter Seven

## Access the Meat

### Choosing the Level of Interaction in Violent Conflict

One of the key features of the sociopath is that he sees everyone as essentially the same—a piece of meat to be butchered. Sociopaths look at everyone this way, regardless of personality, skill, or ability.

You have to keep in mind that sociopaths are not insane. Sometimes they claim to be in an effort to lower their sentence. But that's what's so chilling about many serial killers: they are completely sane people who made rational, calm, cold-blooded decisions to rape and murder and do whatever else they came up with. Ted Bundy, America's most notorious serial killer, once said: "I'm the most cold-blooded sonofabitch you'll ever meet. I just liked to kill; I wanted to kill." Does that sound like someone who didn't know what he was doing?

The other thing to remember is that sociopaths see violence as a useful tool. In a best case scenario, they aren't even thinking about your pain or humiliation; they're just using the violence the same way they'd use a pencil to write with. In a worst case scenario, they're actually getting a charge from your helplessness—enjoying the sense of power, superiority, and prowess. Pleading and talking won't have much effect on these people because they like what they do. Like Ted Bundy, they pride themselves on being cold-blooded sonofabitches. In an online dating profile, they'd list "murder" as a hobby.

And knowing that, you start to understand why they don't differentiate between victims. It never occurs to a sociopath that he'll get caught, or that someone might be able to stop him. Sociopaths are more than twice as likely as any other criminal to be a repeat offender. They not only don't think they'll get caught, they like what they're doing too much to stop. Eventually, every human being looks the same to them: a piece of tender flesh to be brutalized as a means to an end.

A big strong guy with a black belt looks the same to them as a sleeping little girl. The sociopath understands that both their skulls open the same way, their eyes yield to equal pressure, and they both die when their throats are cut.

The sociopath disregards the things that set them apart; he will not interface with their personalities, or the big strong guy's black belt-level skill, or his massive muscles. He will only concentrate on the things that they are both susceptible to.

In order to use violence successfully, in order to have an equal chance of survival, so must you. Don't get caught in the sucker's game of interfacing at higher levels, of showing respect for the person, his skills or physical power. Go straight for the meat.

## The Four Levels of Interaction

### 1. *As a person—social*

This is trying to change behavior, mood, or motivation. It's where most people would like to keep the situation, and in our Happy Place, this is where everyone would want to be, able to talk a serial killer out of his crazy tree.

### 2. *As a skill set—antisocial*

This is trying to outwrestle him, or out-technique him in a 90 mph chess game. This is a duel in which the most skilled practitioner will typically win. It is 'civilized violence' and seen as 'fighting fair.' Some bar fights look like this, especially if they're between drunken friends. School yard fights almost always involve antisocial interactions. So do combat sports: wrestling, boxing, martial arts. Someone might get hurt, but not badly. No one is really meaning to seriously hurt someone else. At worst, they might try to "teach him a lesson." If someone in this type of interaction was seriously injured or died, the other parties would be horrified.

### 3. As an animal (via strength, speed, stamina)—antisocial

This is pitting your strength against his, trying to outmaneuver or outlast him, going blow for blow. This typically looks pretty brutal and ugly. Two lions fighting for dominance of their pride might look like this. In all likelihood, no one's going to die—at least, that's not the idea—but this isn't your typical schoolyard brawl. Kids would run for a teacher, not stand around watching. While an antisocial fight can be somewhat good-natured, an animalistic fight is serious. Both combatants are taking this seriously. They are out to prove who is the best specimen. This is seen as brutish, desperate and decidedly 'uncivilized.'

### 4. As a piece of meat—asocial

This is regarding him as a physical object beholden to the natural laws of the universe. Paying no heed to the person, the skill, or the ability. This is seen as almost universally 'bad'— people who do this naturally are classified as 'evil' in a social setting. This is interfacing with him as a thing that can be broken down and rendered non-functional.

It's interesting to note that these four levels correspond to different ranges and comfort zones:

Interfacing with the person can be done from across the street, a distance from trouble where most people feel safe (they can always take off running if it gets out of hand).

Interfacing with his skill-set is almost always done at a pace away, with the contestants circling to get a feel for the other guy's skill level, feinting and parrying and otherwise dancing around. It's all about giving yourself enough room to see what he's doing and try to counter it.

Interfacing with his physical abilities is done skin-to-skin, but that's as deep as it goes.

Interfacing with the frailties of the flesh is done beneath the skin—true injury is about disregarding the sanctity of the body and simply destroying it.

## What-ifs, Buts and Maybes

As a trainer, I'm constantly interacting with people of various sizes, ages, genders, and skill-levels. What's interesting isn't so much the physical configuration of the person I'm training, but the things they ask me. The kinds of questions people ask during training can tell you a lot about where their head is at and at which level they're stuck on. Most people are used to the social sphere. They accept the antisocial sphere as sometimes necessary, and that's as far as they ever want it to go. Getting them to move beyond that to the asocial can be an incredible challenge. They come up with all sorts of questions to avoid confronting the truth. But the important thing to note is that none of their worries have any impact on injury whatsoever.

## The 'Socialist'

The person who is uncomfortable with the whole idea of conflict will ask questions that dance around the issue from across the street, like, "How can I tell if he wants to hurt me?" and such. It's obvious that they never want to engage in actual violence. Most people start out here. What they're actually looking for is some kind of warning system that will tell them when they should get away. They've yet to realize that what they're training for is the type of violence that can't be avoided. If you have the option to run away, then take it. There's no "how can I tell" involved. How can you tell if he wants to hurt you? You'll know. Your instincts will tell you. And at the time, you won't think about it because it won't matter.

## The Duelist

People trained in martial arts usually get hung-up on interfacing with his skill. They'll ask the most what-ifs, like, "What if he throws a spinning back kick?" "What if he counters my joint lock?" and "What if he's holding the knife like this?" They are also overly concerned with blocking—both in doing it and worrying about having it done to them. These are the tacticians. They want to lay out every scenario beforehand so that when it happens, they have a technique to address it. Trying to explain to them that they have to leave the technique behind is difficult because it's been so carefully drilled into their heads. These people are also concerned with keeping things at the social level. They never want to move outside the world regulated by rules and fair conduct.

## The Animal

Untrained people who can come to terms with the idea of conflict usually end up fixated on physical attributes. For smaller, less athletic people it manifests as worry about how they'll fare against bigger, stronger, faster adversaries; big, strong folks have the opposite problem—they typically believe they cannot be defeated by 'lesser' beings. Both are equally problematic. Violence isn't about prowess. It's about injury. A five foot tall, 100 pound woman is just as capable of gouging your eyes out as a six foot tall, 250 pound man. Don't ever fall into the trap of thinking the stronger party prevails. Whoever gets it right, first, does.

## Sociopaths & Butchers

Almost no one shows up comfortable with injury as a starting point. If someone came in excited about hurting people, I would be very worried.

**Progress**

Another interesting thing to note is that progressing through the levels is not linear. Socialists don't usually walk through the others to arrive at injury. They go one of two ways—either they dig in their heels and cram their heads into the sand and will never, ever cross the street, or they go straight from where they are to injury (though sometimes with a short stopover at the animal level).

Duelists are another thing entirely. It is often very difficult to wean them off of the idea that they need to respect and/or thwart his skill before they can be effective. If they do move on, it's usually with a long stopover at the animal level. His skill bothered them before; now they've transferred that worry to his physical abilities. Those who have taken the long walk from skill to animal to injury are typically the most evangelical about the whole process. (As opposed to those who went straight from social to injury. They usually don't see the whole experience as that big a deal).

Animals are easier to nudge into interfacing directly with the meat of the matter. They're pretty close, conceptually, and they just need to be shown how to direct their efforts away from strong points and into the weak ones. (Instead of going strength-to-strength, go strength-to-eyeball).

If you're reading this I'm going to assume that you don't have a problem with violence in a general sense, that you're not hung up on the social aspects from across the street. So where are your hang ups? What are you stuck on? Are you worried about what he'll do if he's skilled? Or bigger-stronger-faster? Be honest with yourself. You're letting yourself down if you lie—you're not going to get any more effective that way.

If the idea of going after a trained Goliath makes you sweat (more than the usual, healthy amount, I mean) then you need buckle down and study up on injury. Seek out photos of sports injuries (for broken joints and twisted, non-functioning limbs). Autopsy reports from non-firearm killings—especially where the victim was beaten to death—are illuminating. Troll the internet for videos of prison fights and violent muggings. Essentially, look for anything where the survivor is interacting with the other person as a piece of meat.

You'll be repulsed and comforted simultaneously.

# Chapter Eight

## The Hardest Lesson

I'll be honest with you, when the Virginia Tech shooting first happened, I really didn't want to write about it. Not the day it happened, and not the next. Never. I didn't want to write about it because nothing I could say would be novel, or surprising—if anything this incident was just everything we're always saying and doing anyway, knobbed up to 11 and turned on a mass of hapless innocents.

But mostly, I didn't want to write about it because I did not wish to inadvertently speak ill of the dead or laud a mass murderer.

What changed my mind? To a large degree it was the back channel chatter I got—phone calls, emails, PMs from pretty much everyone who knows what I do for a living. Everyone wanted my take on it. The straw that broke the camel's back was one in particular who pointed out what a difference it made, for them personally, when I spoke to the point on the 9/11 attacks the day after they occurred.

That, and the comments of an Israeli lawyer. But more on that in a moment.

I'm going to skip the obvious dissection for the reasons stated above, and instead focus on problems within American society itself that, in my opinion, make it possible for one man with a 9mm pistol to slaughter more than 30 people.

It comes down to two things that together make for a tragic oxymoron: we live in a society that is voyeuristically obsessed with violence, and yet we have very little real information on how to function in violent conflict. To me, this is a lot like living on boats and aggressively plying the seas while not actually knowing how to swim.

On the one hand, our culture celebrates violence in video media, music, and indeed our literature. On the other we recoil from any attempt to confront the realities of violent conflict. I believe most people view portrayals of violence in media through an antisocial lens; when the 'hero' kills a 'bad guy' they are seeing the school yard fight we often talk about.

But the moment one attempts to realistically address violence, and train for it, we're suddenly madmen. You would not believe the amount of static I get for being honest, forthright, and attempting to educate people in this matter. Of course, this is a natural, sane, response; it would make perfect sense if we lived in a perfect world.

And therein lies the problem: if only madmen are allowed and/ or expected to use violence, then only madmen will have access to the tool.

That brings me to the comment from the Israeli lawyer, made to a colleague of mine. He asked, "Why didn't they just rush the gunman?" He further commented that this was the 'tactic of record' in Israel.

Did they try that? I don't know. I fear that what allowed this murderer to work so efficiently was the same thing that allowed the 9/11 attacks to succeed: individual fear of a tool.

The mechanics that make handling the situation are simple. The psychological element is not. In other words, the mechanics of knocking out or killing an armed person are very straightforward. Making yourself get up and get in there—overcoming the terror and chaos in your head—is not.

Knowing the mechanics of this sort of action, and training with them, helps the psychological side immensely. Knowing what to do is its own kind of confidence. Even something as simple as deciding, as a society, that we'll all rush and overwhelm a gunman—having that plan ahead of time—goes a long way toward mitigating individual, paralyzing fear.

Realizing you have no idea what to do can only fuel the terror and give the murderer the time and space he needs to work.

It's already been said, in many places, that a single student armed with a firearm could have made a difference. While they are right, let's tease out the 'why that works.'

Another student with a gun could have affected the outcome because he or she would have held, in their hand, the power to kill. So what's really being said here is that one student who had the power to kill could have made a difference. Whether that power comes from a device or from knowledge of how to do it with their bare hands is immaterial. In fact, any amount of real information as to what to do when suddenly dropped into this situation could have made a difference. But none of us really know anything about violence, in spite of our constant exposure to it. None of us are comfortable enough to know how to kill when the situation arises.

Instead, due to the way our society processes violence, there was only one person there who had access to the tool. If we don't change the way our society processes violence only one person is going to learn anything from all this—the next shooter.

## Don't Flinch, Don't Look Away—Learn

You've heard me say that the one doing the violence prevails, and you've probably seen this adage in action (hopefully only on video). You buy the logic of it, see the truth of it stitched across the entire swath of human history. But have you ever really thought about what that means for you?

In poker they say that if you sit down at the table and don't know who the sucker is, it's you. If you find yourself there, as the sucker, it's best to get out before the first card hits the table.

In violence, if you're not the most dangerous person in the room, you're a potential victim.

So really, the end-goal of all training, all time on the mats, every last millisecond, even reading this book is to become the most dangerous person in the room. Period.

Wherever you go, no matter who you're surrounded by, you need to be the most dangerous person there. The One person who, if you were to be caught on video doing violence, would stand out for directness, ferocity and brutality. The One obvious person in the frame who is in control, making everyone else want to get away from them—and breaking people at will. The One who would make even a casual observer blanch and crap their pants.

**You want to be the center of the storm.**

Right now you're all nodding in agreement. You got it, this is nothing new. That's you to a 'T.' It's where you live, it's how you roll, because you're dedicated to living an embarrassingly long life and dying in bed surrounded by your geriatric great-grandchildren with your third baboon heart beating in your chest.

Here comes the hard part, the hardest lesson, because violence has nothing to do with being dedicated to living—it has everything to do with being dedicated to hurting, crippling and killing people. With being The One person there who wants to do those things more than anyone else in the room.

Who do we know of who pulled off this trick recently?

That's right—the Virginia Tech shooter.

His use of the tool of violence was stunning in its base utility—it was textbook. So much so it is now your required reading.

I already told you that I don't want to applaud this guy. I don't want you to think that I approve of what he did. Hell, I'd like to not lay it out like this at all, but then the question becomes 'when?' There will never be a good time, so like a nasty-tasting medicine we're just going to get it over with.

He was everything I laid out in the above paragraph, the one you were nodding enthusiastically to just a moment ago. Feels different now, doesn't it?

If you really got it, if you really understood what we're up to and up against here, it wouldn't feel different at all. You would nod, but not enthusiastically. You'd do it with a grim determination.

See, it's kind of cool to whisper to yourself, "I'm The One, the most dangerous person in the room." Kind of puffs you up, makes you feel like a 007 agent.

The reality of that statement ain't so nice—or socially acceptable. Because what you're really saying is "I'm like the Virginia Tech shooter."

The center of the storm, with unflinching intent, making everyone want to get away from you rather than go after you, delivering multiple injuries per person, dropping them and then making sure they don't get up.

If you had read the preceding paragraph before I mentioned Virginia Tech, you'd think it was pretty cool. You'd think, "That's me." But not now. Now you're wrestling with it. Sickened by the idea.

That's why it's the hardest lesson.

It's not only hard to learn—most people don't want to learn it.

If you're having trouble with it, then that's your biggest problem with training for violence—not how good or bad your technique is, or where exactly is the spleen target or not knowing enough joint breaks.

Because if you walk into the room and you don't know who the most dangerous person there is, it sure as hell isn't you.

# PART THREE:

# PUTTING THE PRINCIPLES INTO ACTION

# Chapter One

## Roadblocks, Plateaus & Epiphanies

In thinking about how it felt to learn and process the tool of violence for my own use, I realized there were five distinct phases in the evolution of my thinking and, by extension, my training focus. As my understanding grew, the way I trained changed. Or, I should say, as my understanding became more simplified and streamlined, so did the way I trained.

**Phase 1: Approaching the material from a fantasy angle.**

I originally came from a martial arts background, and so approached the new material as merely a 'super-rugged' martial art. Or all martial arts crammed into one. We all bring our own appetite to the table; an all-in-one approach is what I was seeking on my martial arts Vision Quest because that is what I'd been led to believe was required when someone wants to kill you.

I was also well 'informed' by the mass media. I was sure that the real-deal would go down like the climax of a Schwarzenegger film. I was looking to square off and trade blows until I could pull out a really cool technique and impale my foe on a protruding fuel rod from a nuclear reactor. And then coolly declaim a pithy one-liner. Really.

I wanted to train for a duel, and was acutely interested in countering whatever it was he had in store for me and being able to get in. What exactly would happen in there? I had no real idea. But I did have the fantasies.

My mat time reflected my thinking; I wanted to look cool with all kinds of whippy-spinny crap. I went fast and slapped my reaction partners around. I probably wasn't a lot of fun to work with.

## Phase 2: A more realistic angle, but not quite.

I realized that movies and comic books were crap when it came to useful instruction in violence—they require violence to be dramatic and climactic for effect. Real violence, in contrast, was often nasty, brutish, and short.

All that realization did for me was make me aware of my own insufficiencies; it made me overly troubled by what the other guy was up to. I sought to prepare for all contingencies. I worked over scenario after scenario in my head, trying vainly to cover every 'what-if.'

I sought ultimate, unassailable superiority as a palliative to my anxiety. I worked hard on 'advanced' techniques, i.e., ever fancier joint breaks and throws.

This phase could also be called minor paranoia. This was a huge breakthrough moment, both triumphant and terrifying. If you've engaged in combat sports, you might know the feeling: you finally move up a level, and you feel a huge rush of pride together with a twinge of fear. Now you'll go from fighting guys at your level to much tougher, harder opponents; in a single moment, you've gone from king of the hill to bottom of the barrel.

That's a human condition, by the way. It happens to kids graduating from junior high school: it's a huge accomplishment to pass grade nine and head over to that big brick building, but you've just gone from being the biggest, toughest kids in school to the youngest and smallest. Any triumph usually comes with new challenges, just to make things more fun.

When you realize that "real" violence is nothing like what you see in the movies—that it's brutal, tough, scary, and usually over in an instant—that's one of those moments. It's a huge victory. You've finally overcome years of social programming and seen the truth. At the same time, though, it's absolutely terrifying, because now you know what's out there. And if you're anything like me, that leads to this kind of frantic training, a desperate desire to make sure you know how to handle what you might come up against.

**Phase 3: Realizing he's not my problem—I'm his problem.**

It's great to say it—it's another thing entirely to live it. I knew it was true, but I was still not comfortable owning that ideal. I had a better grip on what was up but I was still plagued with nagging concerns over what he might be up to. It was a lot of 'okay, I got that, but what if...'

This was the first time in my training where I began to concentrate on injuring the man as a priority above and beyond what he was doing or what I thought would look cool. My mat time started to get ugly in the good way.

In other words, the transition ended. I overcame the shock of my initial realization about the true nature of violence and began to deal with it. Let's face it: people can adapt to almost anything. We get used to living without people we love who have died, we get used to wars and starvation and just about anything else. It's completely natural that, sooner or later, we'll get used to the truth.

Of course, before you get used to anything, you have to encounter it. The whole point of this book is that we want you to encounter violence, real violence, as an idea before you meet it on the streets. That way you can go through your moment of shock and fear, get over it, and be fully prepared for what you have to do when you meet violence face to face.

**Phase 4: Arriving at the singularity of violence.**

This is where it all came together. This is where I realized that all the seemingly disparate elements of violence were really just aspects of the same thing—all strikes, joint breaks, and throws, with and without tools, were all the same thing. Injuring the man. This is where I made the shift from 'fighting' into 'injuring.' And it only took me 11 years!

This change came, to a large degree, from nine years of teaching. But it also came from anxiety fatigue. I was tired of worrying. I was tired of getting all wrung out in knots over every little thing that might could go wrong. The possibilities for fatal screw-ups were infinite; in the end it was just easier to let that all go and focus on breaking the man. I realized I was my own worst enemy and decided to chuck it all and become the thing I feared most:

A person so narrowly dedicated to destruction that only death could stop me.

While dispatching the 'bad guy' with flair and uncounterable aplomb is a nice idea, it's nowhere near as good as walking away with your life. A solid, pedestrian money shot to the groin is worth 10,000 of the fanciest techniques.

I began to own and live the truth that all targets are equal, as are all injuries; my workouts slowed and became inexorable. I simply took what I wanted. I laughed with unrestrained pleasure when people tried to grapple me. I taunted them openly as they tried to pin me, "Are you sure you got me?" Then I grabbed them by something unexpectedly fragile and dragged them screaming into my serial injury cave. Eyes and mouth wide, fingernails splintering on the stones as they vanished into darkness.

It was all about me all the time, and I was never sorry again.

### Phase 5: Approaching the material from a sociopathic angle.

Most people would probably prefer not to be classified as sociopaths. That's fair enough. I don't think of myself as a sociopath, either. But in order to understand violence, you have to look it the same way a sociopath would. That's the only way you'll ever stand on even ground, predator-to-predator.

The moral of the story? In the end, it's just as simple as this:

It's not about what he's got or what he wants to do—it's about getting over there and breaking him.

So what's this mean for you?

It took me 11 years to get to this point because there was no one there to tell me any different. I'm here to tell you how it goes down right now, to give you the tools to make it work and show you how to swing those tools. You get the benefit of every last second I spent on the mats, every last second I spent thinking about it. Instead of making you relive every second I spent, I'm here to give you the end result. I'm here to tell you different. Instead of reinventing the wheel, all you have to do is grab a body and hit the mats.

# Chapter Two

## Training For Life

*"People often say that motivation doesn't last. Well, neither does bathing—that's why we recommend it daily."* —Zig Ziglar

Something we frequently hear is, "Okay, I get this whole violence thing, but what if—" followed by some hypothetical situation you've come up with that might go down on the streets.

This is code for 'I don't want to get hurt.'

Well, nobody does. If this were something that you could reliably choose to avoid, it would be a central part of our training. But it isn't.

The truth about violence is that you're going to get punched, kicked, stabbed, whacked and shot—whether you're the 'winner' or not. Any other outcome—like walking through it and putting your man (or men) down without getting a scratch on you—is pure luck.

What you can realistically expect as the survivor is to limp out of there alive.

Accepting the reality of the situation ahead of time will save your life. It'll keep you from quitting right at the point where things are at their worst. Let's say you are trained in 'knife defense.' And then you get stabbed. Your first though will be 'I screwed up' which will lead to the result of 'screwing up': death. You'll be thinking about the result of your mistake—'I'm going to die!'—instead of what you need to be thinking to survive, primarily 'take the eye.'

Look at the difference there. We have an abstraction versus a concrete action. Which one do you want coming out of you when your life depends on it? You've heard it said that there are no atheists in a foxhole. Well, there are no philosophers in a knife fight. Not live ones, anyway.

It's also important to note that the people who are best at violence completely ignore the 'what's he up to' side of the equation; they simply put all their effort into making violence one-sided and keeping it that way. They wade in and get it done, to the exclusion of all else.

And so should you.

Success is your benchmark. You are going to do your best to model the efforts and behaviors of those who are successful at violence. In short, you're going to act like the survivors.

You're obviously not going to act like the dead (that goes without saying), nor are you going to model behaviors and action that you might wish were present. Rather than accessing violence the way you wish it worked, you'll look to reality for your training cues.

This is a huge leap into uncomfortable places.

Instead of training the way you wish it were, you're going to train the way it is. You're going to start at the point of injury, and let the other guy worry about waiting and seeing. He can wait and see what you're up to while you do it to him.

Reality is a smog-belching bulldozer with the elves and fairy-folk of nice ideals all broken and snarled up in its iron treads. If you have a choice—and you do—then train to put yourself in the driver's seat, and the other guy beneath the blade.

## Three Common Training Mistakes

Let's assume for the moment that you're with me. You understand that real violence is asocial, scary, and deadly, and you know that you have to train to be prepared to attack and kill. How do you go about doing that?

Well, first let's talk about how not to do it—these are the three most common training mistakes practiced by many self-defense and martial arts experts:

## 1. Training for one-on-one combat.

I've hammered home the importance of the cold hard fact: "you do what you train." Anything you do in a training environment is exactly how you are conditioning yourself to respond in a life-or-death situation. Most of my clients understand this principle in applying trauma to the body. They are careful to insure that they strike with a tight fist or make sure that they complete the rotation of their body to deploy maximum force upon the given target area of the other guy.

However, even if you do all this, you won't be prepared to face more than one opponent. You'll be excellent at handling the one guy, but add in another and watch the meltdown occur. And the simple fact is, there's safety in numbers, even for the criminal sociopath. People tend to attack in groups.

You must always treat every confrontation as having multiple guys. You need to be instructed how to be a 360° fighter and to be aware of your surroundings at all times. In TFT, all fighting is against multiple guys even in a one-on-one training session. This means as I take out my current victim I'm aware of my surroundings and hunting for my next victim If you've never really trained for multiple guys then you've never trained for life-or-death confrontations. Don't make that mistake.

## 2. Wasting time "conditioning" your body.

Martial artists are amazing. They can do extraordinary things. I've seen television shows where they bend spears with the hollow of their neck, sit on the floor in a cross-legged position while ten students attempt with 'all their might' to push the master over, and a variety of others who could pass needles through their skin without bleeding, cut themselves, then 'miraculously' stop the bleeding, put sharp objects in their eyes, etc., etc.

It's impressive, all right. Unfortunately, conditioning the body to take a hit is also a complete waste of time. "Why?" you ask?

Simply because violence is so unpredictable. I can almost guarantee that the area of your body you chose to 'condition' will not be the area attacked in a real situation. More importantly, there are over 70 anatomical areas of the human body that provide some 200 specific targets that cannot be 'conditioned.' As you can see, it's very easy to injure the human body just by knowing a small number of these 200 options. (Really, any single one will do if you know what to do with it.)

You can't condition the body for real violence, and neither can those people listed above. Don't be impressed with parlor tricks.

To the guy putting a sharp object in his eye—offer to do it for him (just be prepared to stab him in the eye).

For the guy bending the spear with his neck—step behind him and shin kick him to the groin, then watch how easily the spear pierces his throat!

For the guy sitting cross-legged and having everyone attempt to push him over—take your fingers and dig them straight up under his chin and watch him topple over.

Finally, the sword swallower—I guarantee if you take your fingers and jam them down his throat, he will gag and puke just like everyone else.

The point is this: the human body can be trained to handle trauma to a specific area under controlled conditions. This has nothing to do with creating injuries. Take away the controls, and chaos reigns.

That's why attempting to control the uncontrollable is a very poor use of your time. With proper targeting, on the other hand, you get injuries regardless of the other guy's size, strength, speed—or ability to bend spears with his neck.

Remember: the best way to survive a violent encounter is to be the one doing the violence.

### 3. *Relying on training tools.*

Many people firmly believe in training tools like punching bags. They may agree that a bag can't take the place of a live partner, but they point out that you can hit a bag harder and more often than you can a human being, thereby developing strength, speed, and stamina.

This is true for competition training—but training for competition is not the same as training for violence. Such aids are counterproductive when your focus is violence.

In the late 1980s I remember reading a very interesting interview with a former San Diego police officer. He started his career in the 1920s when San Diego still retained some of its 'Wild West' reputation (and the problems associated with that 'reputation').

In this interview the officer tells numerous stories of putting down riots and engaging in all methods of hand-to-hand combat in order to 'do the right thing.' That was all very entertaining, but what struck me was what he told the interviewer midway through the article.

He said that prior to joining the department he had been a boxer and really enjoyed going to the boxing gym. He loved sparring and working out on the heavy and speed bags. But he found that the more he dealt with criminals on the street the more his boxing worked against him. He noted there was different 'timing' on the street and people 'moved when you hit them.' It got to the point where he had to stop boxing because it made him slower on the street.

The interviewer was stunned by this statement and questioned him further. The officer then elaborated saying that it was a lot easier to hurt people when you didn't have to 'box.' What you had to learn instead was to stay on top of them as you hit them.

I remember one example where he told how easy it was to break a neck after you hurt a man as long as you moved past him while doing it (remember this was the '20s). He demonstrated how he did this to the interviewer saying it was a great way for a couple of cops to quickly put down a riot.

Hmmm ... sounds an awful lot like getting your first injury, then doing a joint break, all using penetration and rotation—where have you heard that one before?

Bottom line: Competition training aids like heavy bags are poor preparation for doing violence against another human. The bad habits ingrained with such products can rob you of opportunities to end the situation you find yourself in NOW, instead giving the other guy time to recover and do violence on you.

## Principles of Target-Focus Training

I received an excellent breakdown of TFT's training principles from a client one day. They're worth sharing with you now because these are exactly the things you need to keep in mind when you're training for real life—not the boxing ring. They are:

## Violence Basics

- Work like a sociopath in a life-or-death confrontation—maim, cripple or kill.
- There are no rules in violence—remove any such boundaries or you will suffer the consequences.
- Your only weapon is your brain. Everything else is a tool.
- In violence, never focus on the other guy's tools (gun, knife, or club). Focus on taking out his weapon (brain)—simply taking away the tools and leaving the other guy functional may cost you your life.

- Violence is not give and take—make it one-sided.

## Doing Violence

- Be the one doing the violence.
- Aim small, miss small.
- Always focus on striking targets.
- Always strike, never block.
- Have a first strike mentality: don't hesitate.
- Always strike as hard as you can, with your entire body.
- Never quit until the other guy is nonfunctional.
- Always assume multiple persons in a violent confrontation.
- Always ask yourself "what is available to me" NOT "what is being done to me?"

## Social vs. Asocial

- Don't use violence to solve social situations.
- Don't ever posture with violence.
- Don't try to 'teach someone a lesson' or you may get schooled.
- Walk away from ego-based confrontations—there is no threat.
- If you can use social skills to avoid violence do so, but if it is asocial then there is only one option: violence.

## Training for Violence

- Be brilliant at the basics.
- You do what you train: make sure you train for the real world.

All in all, a pretty good primer for violent conflict. I was glad to see our training had made sense to him and sunk into a deep enough level that he was able to order the basics in his own words, for his own use. His list made it obvious to me that he'd taken ownership of the material—that he had the tool of violence firmly gripped in both fists.

What he's unrolled here is a great blueprint for anyone to get started building the tool for themselves. You can't go wrong with any of it; it's a to-the-point distillation of why criminals are successful, and how you can be, too.

# Chapter Three

## Learn To Fight or Work Out?

*"There is a great streak of violence in every human being. If it is not channeled and understood, it will break out in war or in madness."* —*Sam Peckinpah*

I saw a commercial for one of those dance instruction programs that guarantees you'd be able to dance as well as any member of the most popular boy-bands. The program showed a group of students following the instructor step-by-step to learn some pretty complex moves, choreographed to perfection.

The result was that by memorizing the steps and combining the moves, students could mimic the formerly difficult routine.

It reminded me of watching a Wushu team practice their show. For those of you that aren't familiar, Wushu is a Chinese martial art that is delivered via a stage performance. The fights are very elaborate and it takes a great deal of practice to put on a convincing show.

As I watched the team practice it was interesting to note that whenever someone wanted to screw around all they had to do was execute a move different from the routine. Literally you would be watching a fight scene you'd swear was pitting two highly trained fighters in mortal combat when all of a sudden one of the guys would move differently ... maybe slap the other guy in the face like the Three Stooges used to do. Everyone would laugh, then take a break. But that slap also woke me up out of the dream state I was in as I watched the performance.

I realized that this was exactly the method in which most martial arts or combat sports are instructed. Especially when they try to train for self-defense. Basically there are set patterns you memorize in response to various staged attacks. Memorize those responses and you can look pretty impressive.

But what happens if you vary the attack?

Most students freeze.

Why?

Because they were never taught how to fight!

Nope, they basically were taught to dance—and as long as everything went according to the routine, they could do okay. But we all know things never go exactly as planned.

Fighting is no different—whether you are on the mat at your training center or on the street locked in mortal combat with the other guy(s). The only variation is that when you fight with your training partner you don't actually maim, cripple or kill. You still target and simulate those exact strikes, just at a pace your partner can handle.

If, however, you're operating in a 'training' mode where you are memorizing a 'set' response to an attack, you are learning nothing but a 'dance' move. Such training is coordination training, not fighting. If you don't know the difference, you can easily fall victim to the "now-it's-for-real" syndrome. That's where you face an imminent attack, yet hesitate ... as your brain tries to accept the fact that "this is for real."

Contrast this to the well-trained fighter who simply sees all this as merely fighting and proceeds to: a) find his targets and b) strike. The only difference to the fighter is the fact he can now strike with full power. That's because the well-trained fighter never sees himself as 'training'—he's always fighting. Understand this concept and you'll always be prepared ... no matter what the situation.

### Fighting is Fighting, Not Getting In Shape

I meant what I said: the well-trained fighter sees everything as a fight. He'll never tell you he's going to "workout" when he heads for a training session. That's because the emphasis isn't on "working," it's on the fight itself.

While I was shooting a new video series, my friend (and world class Olympian strength coach) Charles Staley was hanging out and watching. At one point one of the instructors asked Charles about how to improve his workout regime to get a better body composition.

The instructor made the comment, "What sucks is once you know how to take people out, there's no motivation to get big."

Now, I wouldn't necessarily agree with that statement, but I understand what he meant—using violence as a survival tool and staying in shape have nothing to do with each other. There are obvious health and lifestyle benefits to being in good physical shape but that is not a condition for effectively using violence to injure an asocial criminal.

Violence is achievable by everyone—not just those in good shape.

That's the realm of combat sports and martial arts where being in shape is important. Rules hinder your ability to use violence effectively and when competing, the goal is to better your opponent skill-wise, not injure him and leave him nonfunctional. Physical conditioning can often be the defining factor in such contests, especially with two equally skill opponents.

Using violence requires intent. You have to model asocial conditions to recognize when to act. Effective targeting allows you to maximize the use of violence. This allows you to bypass the need for good physical conditioning to be able to create injuries on any human body regardless of the size, speed, and physical strength of the other guy.

My point is that violence is available to everyone regardless of physical condition. TFT helps you to learn how to use violence most effectively ... but you don't have to know TFT to use violence to protect yourself.

Again, the prisons are full of 'untrained' murderers who already understand this point. Don't use the excuse you need to get in shape as a reason not to understand the tool of violence.

**Worry About What Matters**

Some people come to TFT looking for an exercise program. When I tell them to work on targeting, it baffles them.

I tell people over and over the best way to hit harder is first hit your targets. I also give people a simple drill: to constantly look for targets throughout their day as they see people in the streets, malls, grocery stores, etc. The best way to improve a skill is to constantly practice it in non-stressful settings. That way under stress the brain naturally seeks out this familiar skill set. Professional athletes throughout the world use this visualization method—and the better they are at it, the better their performance.

Yet over and over, I get confused looks and people saying, "Ok, I'll do that, but what type of workout should I do?" They want me to give them a weight-based workout to improve their power and (most won't admit) their body composition.

I laugh to myself and wonder why they even asked for my advice. Since I told them to first work on their targeting, perhaps they should ask themselves why I advised that course of action.

The answer? Well, nobody likes to hear it, but it's because **their targeting sucks.**

The biggest improvement they could make in their fighting at this stage is simply improving targeting. Period. After that is accomplished I can then assist them in improving their physical dynamics to increase the trauma they deliver to those targets.

If you want an exercise program, go to the gym. I'm not recommending against that, either; I think it's a great thing to get in shape, and I encourage everyone to maintain physical fitness. But this is a completely different issue from using violence as a tool. Your physical fitness levels are literally nothing compared to your ability to hit a target.

# Chapter Four

## Dead Men Tell No Tales Or,
## Why You Can't Learn Anything of Value
## From the Dead Guy

When we see an act of violence, we feel it in our guts. Our eyes turn to the hapless victim, desperately trying to defend himself, and a part of us is there, suffering with him. This is what sane, socialized people experience when they see violence—empathy. Keep in mind again here that I'm talking about real violence. Yes, people will cheer and jeer at a barroom brawl or a schoolyard spat, but no one cheers when they see a man stabbed in the neck. We can imagine the pain and we empathize with the plight of the victim. This is normal and natural and good. It's what makes society tick along and keeps us from tearing out each other's throats at the drop of a hat.

If you spend any time at all worrying about things like violence, that knee-jerk empathy morphs into questions: What could the victim have done differently? How can I keep that from happening to me? You have a natural tendency to identify with the victim because, let's face it, that could have been you. You're not the one prowling the streets looking for trouble. You're much more likely to be attacked than to be attacking. So the fantasy is that if only you could learn from his mistakes, then what happened to him can't happen to you.

A neat idea, but much like the dead guy, full of holes.

The only piece of (almost) useful information we can learn from the dead guy is to not be there. I say 'almost useful' because it's stupid-obvious. It works okay when you're presented with a clear-cut choice—do I escalate or disengage? But it's stupid when you think about scenarios like workplace shootings: "I'm not coming in today—I feel a shooting coming on."

Anything you think you could learn from the dead guy's performance—if he'd just gone for the eye or not stepped back—is pointless because it's all pretend. It's make-believe.

It didn't happen that way.

Someone else in the picture was doing something. Something that worked. Something that got the job done. Something that made the dead guy dead. He's the one you're going to want to look at if you want to learn what works in violence.

Is this a nice, comfortable idea? Hell no. The vast majority of violent video footage also happens to be criminal. And you, not being a criminal, will find it naturally difficult to empathize with the person doing the violence. But that's the only place where there is anything useful to be learned.

Why? Because it is a record of what works in violence. It's not pretend, it's not coulda-woulda-shoulda—it is. When we shift focus off of the dead guy and onto the survivor we leave the world of conjecture and land squarely in the realm of fact. If you're going to bet your life on something, I don't recommend you bet it on a bunch of opinions or armchair quarterbacking—bet it on the facts.

The person doing the violence is using the facts to his advantage. Pay attention to what he's up to. The only thing the dead guy can show you is the end result of those facts. And that's information you already had going in.

# Chapter Five

## The Final Word in Context—MURDER

Every time I discuss Target-Focus Training or my take on violence, I encounter confusion about what it is I do—confusion that I am, quite frankly, tired of hashing and rehashing. Every time I start a new session, I have to tread carefully so I don't make people think I'm training them to become sociopaths. There are deep-seated biological, psychological and societal reasons for this confusion—and so it is perfectly natural for this confusion to persist—but as an instructor it frustrates me because treading back and forth across this well-worn rut doesn't make you any better at doing violence.

The only thing that makes you any better is getting the mechanics down pat—how and where to cause injury, and how to best take advantage of the last injury you caused. Everything else is just mental masturbation that feels important because it tastes like philosophy with a little bit of work mixed in. You think you're working while avoiding doing any of the real work that will make you better at doing violence—namely, getting a reaction partner and hitting the mats regularly. It's like trying to learn how to fly from a book and then declaring yourself a qualified pilot. You may be book-qualified, but I sure don't want to get up in a plane with you until you've got a few hours of actual on-the-job instruction under your belt. Violence is the same.

This might feel like I'm flogging a dead horse, but my goal is to flay it to the bone (or finally sell it off if you take the original meaning); I want to take it to its absurd, logical conclusion beyond which there is no more jaw-flapping:

What we teach is violence, which is what you need to do when someone wants to murder you.

"So where's the confusion?" you ask. That seems pretty clear-cut. And that's what I think, too. But then the questions start:

Why would I ever need to know how to kill someone?

Won't I get in trouble if I use this in a bar fight?

But what if he's got X and/or Y and he's coming at me like so?

How do I do it to someone who knows what you guys know? What if he does it first?

Or any one of an infinite number of variations. All of these questions tell me one single thing: you don't really believe that bigger-faster-stronger doesn't matter. You want to believe, but you don't.

Where does all the confusion come from? It arises because you think you know what you're seeing, and you're looking at it through the wrong mental porthole. When fists and feet are flying, you see monkey politics. You see competition. It's all Great Apes working out dominance and submission. Don't feel bad—you're hardwired to recognize and respond to this. It's only natural. Which is why I want to start the violence conversation off with one guy shooting another guy to death.

Watching one person kill another with a firearm won't ping your monkey brain. It'll go far deeper, down into the lizard-level, the primeval predator level. You'll see it for what it is —killing. If we look at the underlying mechanics we have all it really is: kinetic energy delivered through anatomy, wrecking it.

And now we have the perfect model to work backwards from. Keep the killing context, keep the wrecked anatomy in mind and now look at other ways of affecting that outcome: kinetic energy delivered through anatomy, wrecking it

So, a fist, a boot, a pipe, a shin, etc., etc., it doesn't matter what as long as it's doing the work that a bullet does, if only in a generic sense. So now if we line up a series of killings and look at them

153

side-by-side, a shooting, a bludgeoning, a knifing, getting hit by a car—we should be able to see the clear, underlying principles that govern all of these equally and immutably. Learning how to wield these principles is the 'getting the mechanics down pat' I mentioned earlier.

All clear, right? No, back to the confusion: everyone gets the gun and the car, but they feel iffy about the pipe and the knife, and downright scoff at the fist, boot, or shin. I don't mean that they object to using them. I'm talking about learning to see them as threats. Everyone knows a gun can kill you, but people think that a knife gives them an element of chance—and they know they can avoid getting killed by a punch if they're careful. What they know is wrong, of course, but they still believe it.

Why?

Because they read it with their monkey politics filter and think there's something they can do about it: "I can't dodge bullets but I can block a punch." This is the ultimate in hubris and sends you down a negative feedback spiral: if you can 'handle' a punch, then of course he can 'handle' it when you're trying to do it to him. You're pissing in your confidence reservoir and your training will look hesitant and spotty. And that's exactly where your skill will go. You're thinking that you're fighting when we really want you doing something completely else.

Let's face the facts: people get stabbed to death. People die from punches to the head. You can beat a person to death. Just because a guy doesn't have a gun doesn't mean you should take him lightly. And the converse of that is true, too: just because you don't have a gun doesn't mean you can't take him down.

I'm trying to teach you how to kill murderers. Everything that fits that narrow model benefits you. Anything that sounds out of place or silly in that context is nothing but crap.

That's why 'murder' is the final word in context. Almost no one knows what to do when that's what's up. 'Fighting' and 'defense' are worthless in that arena—remember that defense wounds are found on corpses and tell the coroner that person 'fought for their life'. You're not going to fight anyone for your life. You're going to kill a murderer.

Armed with this 'new' context, let's look at the common questions:

### 1. Why would I ever need to know how to kill someone?

If that someone is a murderer, then ipso facto. It's like asking, "If drowning can kill me, why learn how to swim?" No one learns to swim and then thinks, "Great! Now I can go get myself in a stupid situation, nearly drown, and use this swimming ability!" No, the swimming is a safeguard for something you hope will never happen. The ability to kill is the same. You don't run off to try it out. You hope you'll never have to use it. But if the situation comes up, the skill is there to save your life.

### 2. Won't I get in trouble if I use this in a bar fight?

Yes. Yes, you will.

### 3. But what if he's got X and/or Y and he's coming at me like so?

[Cue sarcasm] Then you should act enraged and execute a bluff charge and pray he's playing by the same rules—that he's spoiling for a fight and not a murder. Would you ask the same question with a firearm or a steering wheel in your hand? Of course you laugh, but a crushed throat and a gouged eye don't care if it was bullets, hood ornaments or boots that did it. So why should you?

### 4. How do I do it to someone who knows what you guys know?

Injured is injured, dead is dead, regardless of talent or

training. This is back to the bigger-stronger-better thing. Most criminals do know what I know. It doesn't matter. You won't be thinking about that at all—you'll just be looking for an opportunity, causing an injury, and moving on.

### 5.  *What if he does it first?*

Then you have nothing to worry about.

### 6.  *Bigger-faster-stronger?*

The murderer doesn't care who's the biggest, fastest, or strongest—in fact, that's one reason why he's successful. And that should inform your thinking on the subject.

Here's the bottom line: check yourself and stick with what matters. Is your question, your doubt, your worry rooted in the mechanics of injury or is it stuck in monkey politics, in 'fighting?' Be honest with yourself. If it's the mechanics, I can work on that, show you what to do, how to do it. After that it's on you to hit the mats with a partner and take ownership of it. If it's competition, monkey politics, or has anything to do with communication or changing behavior, then it's immaterial and meaningless in the context of killing a murderer.

Because you don't talk to, try to best or even fight with murderers. You kill them.

# Chapter Six

## It's Not About Naughty or Nice

It's about what works & survival. Period.

I was recently reading an article on 'self defense' in which the author was speaking of violence as if you could pick and choose the level of seriousness of the interaction. For instance, he said that if the other guy just wants to 'kick your ass' you kick his ass back, not really hurting him, but teaching him a lesson. If he's a little more serious, then so are you—and if he wants to kill you, well, that's the only time you're going to use certain techniques and targets like eyes, throat and so on.

This idea illustrates a fantasy disconnect between 'fighting' and violence, one that deserves a fantasy name: I often refer to this idea as 'dialing in your Spidey-power.' (With many apologies to Stan Lee).

It's the idea that you can choose to hit someone with, say, 60% of what you've got—and that you'll only ever hit someone with 100% when your life depends on it. It's being able to look at an impending 'fight' and say 'well, he's not really serious, so I'll dial my Spidey-power down to 50%' and then sock him hard, but not too hard, because, after all, you don't want to kill him, right? Of course, this method strongly relies on your latent psychic abilities to figure out the guy's intentions in the split second when he's rushing you. And God forbid you think he's 60% serious when he's giving it 100, because you're going to hold back, and he isn't.

Here's the problem: holding back can get you killed. There are many ways to hold back:

- You can wait and see to try and suss out what his intentions are.

- You can make certain targets 'off limits' because wrecking them is awful (you'll never hear me say otherwise)—like the eyes or breaking a knee, both permanent, crippling disabilities.

- You can 'go easy' on him by not striking as hard as you can.

Any one of these leads directly to reduced effectiveness, poor results, and in the worst case, death—yours, not his.

The idea that you can suss out his intentions is a fantastical delusion. If you don't have psychic powers (and my guess is ... wait for it ... you don't) or know the evil that lurks in the hearts of men like the Shadow does, then you're screwed. You'll know he wants to kill you because, well, he's doing it. That is not the time to find out. In fact, it's never a good time to find out, right? But there's "bad" and "worse," and while he's doing it definitely comes under the heading of worse.

Making targets off limits ahead of time ('I'll never take the eyes') will give you a hesitating hiccup if your next—and only—opportunity is that target. You will stop. And try to get restarted. If you're lucky, it means nothing. If you're unlucky, the opportunity is gone and you just got shot/stabbed/whatever (perhaps again) and you just better hope he got it wrong.

You always want to strike the man as hard as you can. Always—as hard as you can. 'Holding back' reduces the chance of injury. Now we're into the realm of slapping each other around, pissing people off, and delivering nonspecific 'light' trauma that is neither a persistent injury nor spinal reflex inducing. It's wasted motion that lets him know it's on.

Remember the author of that article? Don't worry, he did allow for killing. You see, he figured that in a real worst-case scenario a magical transformation would occur—that even though you'd been neutering and watering-down your training by waiting, making targets off-limits and slapping at them you could suddenly rise to the occasion of your impending murder by crushing the throat or tearing out an eye with full force and effort.

That's a neat idea, but it flies in the face of 'you do what you train.'

So, to that point, how does the way we train serve you? It would seem, on the surface, that we only train for the worst-case scenario, that to use what you know in any other situation would be like using dynamite as a can opener.

Let's put it this way: the 'worst-case scenario' encompasses and includes all other possible scenarios; going in purely to cause serious injury, put the man down and then pile it on (i.e., start kicking a 'helpless' man on the ground) covers, handles and takes care of anything and everything he may have wanted to do to you.

But the real beauty is that you can stop at any time. You'll typically do this the moment you recognize that he's nonfunctional.

Let's say you start out by breaking his jaw at the Temporal Mandibular Joint. You get the minimum expected reaction—he turns slightly, somehow keeps his feet. You come back with a shot to the groin and get a huge reaction: he goes down face-first and tries to curl up in a fetal position. You break his ribs and then strike to the side of his neck, knocking him unconscious. At this point you recognize that he is nonfunctional (to your satisfaction) and stop.

Notice that I didn't mention any techniques or tools—that's because they don't matter. Injuries matter.

This sequence could have been different at each node of injury— you break his jaw and he spins around three times and lays down, out cold; you stop when he goes fetal after the groin strike; you stop after breaking the ribs because as far as you're concerned, your read on him is 'done.'

You also know how to carry it to a more final conclusion with a stomp to the neck, a neck break, a stomp to the throat, etc. But always as an informed choice—not out of desperation, and not after having been trained that it is 'wrong' or morally less-than.

You also know how to start right off with throat-eyes-neck break, but again, as a conscious choice. If killing is what will see you through, you will kill him. If killing is not appropriate, you can still operate because you know where the line is.

This is because you are trained in the totality of violence, understanding it for what it is—a single-use tool that does not have an intensity dial on it. You can't make guns shoot 'nice.' And what a bullet does is the purest expression of everything we're ever talking about. All violence is the same.

So what does this mean for you?

First and foremost it means you understand that violence is not a plaything—you won't goof off with it any more than you would with a loaded firearm. This is healthy. It means you won't get sucked into stupid shenanigans (antisocial) thinking you can use what you know without any negative repercussions. It means you're going to be smarter about when to pull it out and use it. This is going to save you tons of wear and tear, not to mention legal troubles.

It means that when you do use it, you're going to use it the only way you can be sure it works—with no artificial social governors restricting what you can and can't do. You'll strike him as hard as you can to cause injury. And you'll take full advantage of that injury, replicating it into non-functionality.

If we view this through a social lens it is savage, brutal, dirty, unfair and very probably illegal somewhere. This was the essential thesis of the self-defense author. But the question you have to ask yourself is are you going to bet your life the other guy is playing by the rules?

If he is, well, then you're a jerk, aren't you?

If he isn't, you're dead.

The moral of the story is: screw around with violence the same way you'd screw around with a firearm—don't.

## Knowing the Stakes and Acting Accordingly

Ah, yes. Knowing the stakes and acting accordingly...

... is a ton of crap.

Let me rewind a little bit.

The concept of the universality of violence is a key idea that we come back to time and time again; that is, we treat all violence as equivalent, with no such thing as 'blank' fighting, e.g., ground fighting, knife fighting, stick fighting, etc.

The reason we have to keep coming back to it is because a lot of the time you don't treat it as equivalent; add a firearm, for example, and you think the stakes are different and suddenly want your performance to reflect 'how serious' you believe situation has become.

Sometimes you think it's just social status at stake, or mere wounding. But when the knife or the gun comes out, then it's different, right? Now you're playing for keeps, and so you have to get all serious.

Now you know the stakes, and want to act accordingly.

I call bullshit.

Let me put it this way: you really don't want to know the stakes. You never want to find out if it was life or death, because you know how you'll know? When he's killing you, that's how. That's a stupid, behind-the-curve way to find out. It'll be the last thing you ever know. At that point the information will do you no good. It's like the balance of power between nations: the last thing you want is to realize your enemy has nuclear missiles because they're launching them at you. If you know ahead of time, you'll act to prevent that possibility. But when you're in an actual asocial violent situation, there is no way to know ahead of time—so you have to proceed on the assumption that the worst is true.

If your mat time is focusing on the idea that he's 'empty-handed' and so the stakes are a mere beating, you're probably being sloppy with distance and penetration—letting him have too much of the former and not doing enough of the latter. Then, when you add a firearm into the mix, now it's on, right? Everything changes; you have to tighten up, 'get serious', etc.

You know what you're really doing? You're training to get yourself killed.

Every time you go physical it's for keeps. Every time you yank out the failsafes and go off on him it's serious. Every. Single. Time.

You need to take every turn you get in training as the 'real deal.' Treat him as if he has a firearm, or a knife—because he just might be armed with something worse. He might be carrying what I carry:

A steel bear trap and a pack of wolves.

I never leave home without them. In fact, they're with me constantly.

Now, you might think I'm being funny or losing my mind and to that I would ask that you review any video of inhuman savagery you can find—as sickening as it is—of killing in war, a murder, a brutal, one-sided mugging. Notice that once it starts, there is no escape. The victim doesn't get the opportunity to do much of anything other than get injured, react, fall, and get torn apart.

This is what I think of when someone asks me if I'm a sheep, a wolf, or a sheepdog. (Actually, the first thing I think of it that I'm a Homo Sapiens, a human being, something much, much worse than any of the above. But then, we're all human and probably far too close to it to see just how incredibly powerful an animal we are. Hands-down the apex predator of the entire ecosystem. But I digress).

So, if I have to pick a different animal, I'll pick the way it feels when I'm on the mats—like a steel bear trap and a pack of wolves. The trap set, powerful springs straining beneath a hasty cover of leaves and forest detritus, and a pack of lean, tawny wolves circling in the shadows. Once the trap is sprung, there is no escape—after the steel jaws of the initial strike splinter bone and sunder flesh, the wolves are free to tear the crippled man to pieces.

Why does good training look like this?

Because I know the stakes ahead of time. It's all or nothing, every time. And once that trap is sprung, there is no escape.

Starting right now, here are three things you can do to get there:

### 1. *Throw out the idea that the stakes are variable.*

Treat every turn on the mats as if he has a knife, or a firearm, or, worst-case-scenario, a bear trap and a pack of wolves. Don't get sucked into situational ethics and "what-ifs." You have to assume the worst and deal with the consequences later. Remember, if you actually get into an asocial violent situation it's because everything else has failed. Once you realize you won't be using this stuff in bar fights but against criminal sociopaths, the psychological part gets remarkably easy.

### 2. *Be the steel bear trap and the pack of wolves.*

Once you start, it's all about you. He gets to do nothing but react, fall, and get torn to pieces. He doesn't get to stagger back. He doesn't get to roll away. Get inside and stay there, right on top of him—the maximum distance between the two of you should never be greater than one step/strike. Ideally, you'll be pretty much torso-to-torso the entire time. Make 'there is no escape' your personal violence motto—and then make it a reality.

### 3.  *Work on making universality a reality for you.*

Violence is not a bunch of disparate things all duct-taped together into an unwieldy Frankenmass. It's a singularity. It's just one thing. It has a single use. You can't dial it up and down, 'go easy' or be nice. You do not inflict it upon the 'unarmed' man any differently than you would an 'armed' one. (Think about how dangerous you are, naked. With nothing but your bare hands and intent. As dangerous as a steel bear trap and a pack of hungry wolves, perhaps?)

You need to walk into every free fight session with these three things in mind because you need to act identically in every violent situation—spring the trap and maul at will.

Every training session should feel the same—guns, knives, sticks or not. If it feels different with the gun, if it feels stressful or 'more real', you're missing the point when it's not there—it means you're not taking any of the rest of it as seriously as you should. The obvious, projected intent of the firearm is taking you where you should be all the time when you're on the mats.

Buckle down, focus and free fight to make the tool truly immaterial—get the job done so that it really doesn't matter what he has, even if it's a bear trap and a pack of wolves.

# Chapter Seven

## Time to Stop Lying to Yourself

Experienced instructors are some of the most relaxed people I know.

The question, of course, is why? After all, these are the people who have no illusions about the criminals, sociopaths, and violence lurking around corners. They understand that it's kill or be killed. So why are they so calm about it?

When you have the mechanical ability to cause injury (which you all do) and couple it with the driving motivator of intent, everything throttles back and gets calm and easy—you're not out spoiling for a fight or giving yourself an anxiety disorder by obsessing violently over every human being who brushes up against you.

This is the ultimate goal of every aspect of TFT training: to create a hard knot of intent, ready to pull out and use when the situation calls for it. You simply cultivate the skill, and the will to use it, and then sit back and relax into the rest of your life. Should the need arise, you pull out the knot and brain people with it. Then you tuck it back where it belongs and get on with living. (I should note that I'm not talking about a ball of twine here—in my mind it's an infinitely folded tessellation of agony, a world-heavy fist-sized sphere from which no light can escape). You don't walk around brandishing it high over your head, mad-dogging all comers with a halo of purple lightning dancing about your enraged features.

Without intent, without the implacable will to wield the knot, it's not much better than yoga. Physically challenging, yes. A survival skill, no. (As an aside, it's critically important to remember that the criminal sociopath has very little training—a deficit they more than make up for with vast, raging reservoirs of intent).

So why do people have such a hard time with intent? And most importantly, what can you do about it?

People have a hard time with intent for a number of reasons. They 'suffer' from a natural disinclination toward violence, they worry about what the other guy will do, and they think violence is mechanically difficult. These all seem like valid reasons, so let's look at them one at a time.

### 1. *The natural disinclination toward violence*

Not wanting to physically hurt people is healthy, sane, but ultimately an impediment to survival when someone poses the question to which violence is the answer. You need to get over the idea that anything we're up to here is social in nature. This is why it's so critically important that your free fight time is as asocial as possible—no talking, no nervous laughter, no checking your partner's face for feedback. The only time you should be looking at a face is if you're taking an eye out of it.

I'm not talking about getting fired up and 'hating' your partner. I'm talking about dispassion. Lose the emotional triggers—you're not there to communicate, and raging at your partner (or his targets) is still communication. If you're working with your 'war face' you've kicked the social but are busy reinforcing the antisocial. What you really need is to get off the any-social, and get to its absence. That void space is the psychic storage shed of the knot.

### 2. *Worry about what other guy will do*

Let's be blunt. Injured people are completely helpless. Ask anyone who's done it. The first injury converts a fully-functional person into a gagging meat-sack. Every injury after that is like busting apart a side of beef with your boot heels. This is why experienced instructors are so damned relaxed (and courteous, for that matter). This is also why they won't hesitate to be the first one doing it. I drill this truth home time and time again:

injured people can't hurt you, and they can't kill you. In an asocial situation, that's all that matters. It's the ugly truth that no one wants to talk about—about how people really respond to injury, about how when you cause one, you'll know it because what you see next will stick to the inside of your eyelids for the rest of your life.

What's he going to do? He going to break and behave like an injured person. He's going to go to the worst place he's ever been. And you're going to put him there.

The question you have to ask yourself is will you worry about what he's going to do or will you make him worry about what you're going to do? (Hint: pick the one where you survive).

On this same topic, you need to get off the whole 'attacker/defender' merry-go-round. In any violent conflict there's going to be, by definition, at least one person doing it to another. Be that one person. Decide it's you, now, and every time from now. Out there it's always your turn. If you have to think in terms of there being an 'attacker' then it's you.

Choosing to put yourself in second place is not the best strategy for a win, no matter how much we may venerate the underdog. In a 'fair fight' or a contest, the underdog is the hero. In violence, he's dead.

Quit empathizing with the dead guy. You're doing it because you're nice, you're doing it because you're sane. In a social context, it makes perfect sense. In violent conflict your social skills and mores do nothing but prevent you from surviving. Empathizing with the dead guy at the funeral is sane and normal. Empathizing with him when we're all trying to decide who the dead guy's going to be means you're it.

Bottom line: decide who has the problem. Is it you, or is it him?

### 3.  *Believing that violence is mechanically difficult*

Outside of the psycho-social issues, violence is really, really easy. We're all predators; we're all physically built for killing.

Violence is as easy as going from where you are to where he is and putting a single injury in him. The rest is academic.

How easy is it? General consensus says: easier than training. You get to strike as hard as you can, you don't have to take care of him, and it's over so fast you won't even have time to break a sweat or even breathe hard. The only hard part is giving yourself the permission to be inhumanly brutal. Giving yourself the permission to survive. (Personally, I vote for me every time). It's your choice whether you prefer living with the guilt of seriously damaging another human being, or not living at all so a sociopath can have your ball cap.

Thinking that violence is mechanically difficult (and thereby trying to give yourself an 'out' so you don't have to face your own intent problems) is akin to thinking that swimming in the deep end is any different than swimming in the shallow end. Mechanically, it's the same—swimming is swimming—so the difference is all in your perception. In the shallow end, you can touch bottom and can save yourself from drowning by standing up. In the deep end you're on your own—it's sink or swim.

So everyone thinks mat time is the shallow end; there's no risk, you can always 'stand up' when you get into trouble.

That would make the street the deep end—no back-up, no safety net, just swim or die. I'll grant all of that as true. Just remember, always, that no matter where you're swimming, mechanically it's all the same. The idea that there's a difference is an illusion that takes effort on your part to make a reality. Stop feeding the phantoms and just swim.

Intent—your will to cause injury, your drive to get it done—

is completely up to you. You need to start thinking about it now, personally letting go of the things you've kept between the 'you' you love because he's a lovable 'good guy' and the 'you' that can stomp the throats of screaming men.

I can only show you how to mechanically take someone apart—pulling the trigger on it is up to you, and you alone.

## Intent Means As Hard As You Can

Intent is what makes people scary. It's what you instinctively feared in the criminal. It's what society breeds out of we domesticated humans. But what is it, really? It's far too slippery to hold in the mind's eye, an amorphous, ever-shifting gem shrouded in a halo of mist....

And what good is that to anyone?

If you'll bear with me, I'll try to get it to hold still for a moment. Throw some sunshine on the cloudy facets and get them to sparkle for you. I'll do what I can to stabilize the whole thing; gaze into it, into yourself, and get what you can out of it:

Intent is single-minded, goal-oriented focus.

Intent is being focused on injury to the exclusion of all else. From the moment you perceive a threat to the moment that threat is gone, all you care about is causing injury. From the moment he pulls up his shirt to show you a gun or from the moment you hit the ground face-first, you are on target acquisition and destruction. You will find your targets and smash them, never stopping, never hesitating until you get what you want—an injury. And once you get that first one, you'll pile them on until he physiologically buckles under the mass of trauma and you make him capitulate, pass out or die as you see fit. Intent is about what you are going to force him to do. Intent is making violence one-sided as quickly as possible and keeping it that way.

It's not an emotional state—you're not enraged or Hulked-out or seeing red; it's just that out of all the myriad possible things you could do you are going to pick one (injury) and you're going to get it done to the exclusion of all else, over and over again. One target, one injury. Repeat until it doesn't make sense to continue.

Intent is how hard you swing the bat.

Intent is a self-realizing prophecy that cuts both ways: if you think you can do it, you will; if you think you can't, you won't.

If I ask you to kick a soccer ball, how hard you kick it will depend on what you expect to happen. If you believe that the ball is filled with lead shot, then you'll expect it to hurt and won't kick it as hard as you can. In fact, you'll be very reluctant to kick it at all, and your performance will be a reflection of that reluctance. In a word, it'll suck.

If I tell you that if you don't kick it over the fence I'm going to shoot you in the head, your performance will suffer even more. Your preoccupation with a negative outcome will sabotage your efforts. Your mind will not be focused on the task at hand. You'll be worried about living and dying while simultaneously trying to succeed.

Focus on reality, as it stands, not on all possible outcomes. Focusing on things that may or may not be true, or are demonstrable falsehoods, is the 'feeding of phantoms' that we discussed previously. Thinking that there's nothing you can do, or that you cannot injure him, or that you're going to die are all outright lies until proven true. Why put your efforts into your own defeat? It does nothing to aid you in shaping the reality you want. In violence, the reality you want is the one where he's injured. Everything you do must get you there by the shortest possible route. To consider failure is to aid in your own destruction.

Intent is how much of yourself you'll put into getting it done.

Here's a nifty fact that I like to bring up at training seminars: the one thing that all survivors have in common is that they believed they could survive. The circumstances are immaterial, whether it's a crash, drowning, fire, wilderness, or violence. Survivors report time and time again that when they reached the lethal decision point—am I going to live or die?—they all unequivocally, steadfastly chose to live. They believed they could. I've never heard a survivor say 'and then I quit and waited to die.' (Okay, to be fair, I have heard some say that—but they were saved by others who refused to give it up).

Survivors believe they can alter the outcome.

So, back to the soccer ball. If I hand it to you so you can feel how light and eminently kickable it is, and then tell you that our goal for this training session is to see how far you can kick it, then you are free to work on the mechanics of running up and kicking it with your whole being.

This is what we are attempting to do here with TFT. Only instead of kicking soccer balls we're kicking people in the groin.

If you show up with false assumptions, believing that even though you felt the ball and it was indeed light and bouncy it will still hurt when you kick it, or that you are incapable of kicking a ball very far, then anything I do to train you is for naught. You sabotaged yourself before you even set foot on the pitch.

Negative expectations lead to diminished results.

Believing you can do it, expecting to get it done, gets you what you want.

Intent comes down to wanting to cause an injury more than anything in the world.

Focus your mind in that direction, onto that single vulnerable target, and your body will follow suit. You will plow your entire mass through his throat and crush it.

All because of the simple belief that you can do it.

## Building a Better Monster

Invariably, we get questions along the lines of "Okay, I get all that violence stuff—but what if he's bigger/faster/stronger/(your favorite celebrity masher here)/has a knife/stick/gun/three guns?"

That's a great question. Or it would be if that's what they really meant. More often than not people build a monster in their head around a single overarching fear... And that fear is—

Not to be revealed until the end.

In the meantime, let's take a look at some specifics:

When people look at a larger, stronger man what they're really registering is his potential ability to generate power. He could pick you up and throw you across the room, right? Heck, he could probably pick up and throw a Volkswagen. What they ignore is that though he may have more human tissue than you, he's still made of meat. And meat can be butchered.

Fast and skilled fall into the same category—the desire for a duel. This typically comes from people who are worried about 'getting in.' This is particularly funny as I've never seen a prison murder where the participants had any difficulty 'getting in' on each other; I'm sure this idea would make serial killers shrug as well. In short, professionals who use violence in their day-to-day are conspicuously unconcerned with 'getting in.' And so should you be.

But what if he's armed? Well, if I have a knife and he has a knife, I stab the knife, right? Of course not. So why the hell does this make a difference if he has a tool and I'm using fists and boots? It just means you'll beat him to nonfunctional instead of shooting or stabbing him to nonfunctional.

Ah, but now we're getting to the super-secret fear that is hidden at the core of all these questions—these questions are all saying:

I'm afraid he has intent to do what I won't.

Everyone builds a better monster around the idea of superior intent. The bigger/faster/stronger smokescreen is just worry that he's turned up willing to deliver a serious beating that ends in a brutal curbing while you're just there to look the hard boy or have a manly slap-fight. You know, the kind where no one really gets hurt.

The tool, though, now that's different. When he pulls out a labor-saving device whose sole purpose is to rend meat and break bones, well now he's showing superior intent—intent you're worried you can't match. If you're just there to posture and look the part—if you're just there to duel and teach someone a lesson, then what the hell is he up to with that man-mangler? We all know the answer to that.

Everyone recognizes, on a visceral level, that the armed man is displaying intent they don't have.

That's what everyone's afraid of. Superior intent. All the sideways questions, all the building of better monsters is just dancing around this issue—what if he's really here to kill me? I mean, really this time? The recognition that this just might be so, and you can't or won't match it, intent-wise, is the core fear that everyone harbors.

The dull toll of fear echoing in the intent gap is what I hear whenever anyone asks one of these questions. They're not even consciously aware of it. They'll deny it when pressed.

My advice is to build your better monster—bigger, faster, stronger, meaner, armed in a dark alley. Add in a dash of rainy, moonless night. Pile it on.

And then become him.

**Being the Better Monster**

So now you've built your better monster (complete with night-vision goggles and a chainsaw—why not?). Everyone gets the building up part—it's easy—we're all experts in that even before we walk through the door to train. The question is, of course, how does one go about being that better monster?

The short answer is: figure out why you've decided it's going to work for him. And remember what we've discussed: it's not the gun, or his size or speed. So cut all that garbage and really look at this monster you've created. What exactly makes him so damn scary?

And the even shorter answer to that is: INJURY. But you already knew that.

The long answer is: when you build the better monster you've already decided that he's going to do something to you that you're worried you cannot prevent. You assume that this is going to result in a poor outcome for you.

We can pick that apart to find the salient points, the places where you have recognized (consciously or not) several truths about violence:

### 1. He is going to do things to you.

This has two important components—the recognition that he has intent and resides in the cause state. You're right: he is going to do things to you (or at least, he's going to try). This is actually a powerful and empowering recognition—you'll see why in a moment.

### 2. You can't stop what he is doing.

This is recognition that blocking is a sucker's game, that being in the effect state is not nearly as effective as being in the cause state. Again, it sounds like a negative thought (I can't stop him!) but it's really just recognizing a truth: as long as you remain a victim, you're going to remain a victim. Common sense, right?

### 3. Injury will make you helpless.

This is the 'poor outcome' you fear—you get injured, go

down and get more injured in a downward spiral that can only really bottom out with death.

The real trick to make this self-defeating process worth your while is to flip it inside out. You've built your monster, you've figured out why it's going to work for him—now all you have to do is put yourself in the position of this impossible person. Think like the predator you are and resolve yourself to making the realities of violence work for you instead of against you:

- You are going to do things to him.
- He can't stop what you've already done.
- Injury will make him helpless.

Now you see how the two of you are interchangeable—the driver's seat of violence is up for grabs and belongs to the first person to buckle in and romp on the gas. The other guy gets run over and leaves a star on the windshield.

Which leads us, through the clumsiest of segues, to the fact that no one is immune to violence, and what that reality does for him. And can do for you...

People seek training because what they really want is immunity from violence. It's not the idea of doing it they find appealing, but the idea of preventing it. I know this was true for me.

But then we give them an ugly, unpopular truth—nothing can make you immune and you're on your own.

You're either going to injure him, put him down and savage him on the ground or he's going to do it to you. You're not going to have superior, 'no can defend' technique or superhuman abilities. It's just going to be you and your willingness to tear another human being apart. You're very probably going to take a beating in the process, and you can, whether through inaction, miscalculation, or just plain dumb luck end up on the receiving end of the tool of violence.

No matter how hard and long you train, you can be murdered.

This is the bitterest pill to swallow. It leads to all sorts of 'well, what's the point then?' questions. If I can end up just as dead with or without training, why bother? This disconnect is the same one that often occurs for people with firearms—they believe that somehow the gun will 'defend' them, not realizing that they are going to have to shoot the other guy to death to make it work... and it's even worse with knives. It's going to be messy and noisy and scary well beyond what you can imagine. But the end result is, after a fashion, 'defense' in that dead people can't hurt you.

So why bother? Well, prior to training you were rolling dice. We show you how to 'play the game' with loaded dice. So you end up with an edge. You can still drown if you know how to swim, but most people don't say "why bother?" to that because they understand that while drowning is possible for a swimmer, it's much more likely for a non-swimmer. This is the same scenario.

That edge is only going to mean anything if you accept the inborn frailty of your body as you harden your mind to the task at hand—you, crippling another man for life. There is nothing you can do to make your body immune to injury; the only thing you can change is the amount of intent in your head.

It's going to work for him because he wants to cause injury and throws everything he has into making that idea a reality. He has intent.

It's going to work for him because he is acting on the realities of violence as they stand—he is going to use what works and get it done first because he knows no one is immune. He is acting on the fact that he can be taken. This is why he hits first, why he wades in and goes for broke. He knows if he breaks you first, he is far less likely to have any of it done to him. He knows if he waits he's done for.

This is why you fear him. It is also the key to unlocking the power that causes that fear, the key to harnessing it and making his super-scary power your own.

Turn it inside out and wear it instead of having it wear on you.

Be what you fear.

# Chapter Eight

## Scenario-based Training vs. The Hard Knot

When people say 'scenario-based training,' they're actually using a code phrase for 'all the crap that comes before the actual violence.' The yelling, the approach, the grabby man-dance.

Of course, once the violence starts it's all the same old, same old—injury, injury, injury. Pedestrian, predictable, and downright boring.

All the stuff that comes before, all the stuff that people are fascinated with, is, for our purposes, a waste of time. The lead-in to violence for any given scenario is typically antisocial in nature. The questions people have are 'how do I deal with his behavior?' and 'when do I decide to injure him?' You already have the skills to deal with the former—talk him down, capitulate, or get the hell out of there. As for when to tear into someone, that's a personal call you have to make in general terms ahead of time; in specific terms it's based on how you read the situation.

If you recognize a threat and you think you can't live with it, then get busy shutting him off. If you think it's something you can live with—merely antisocial in nature—then act accordingly. Use your social skills, or set a new 100m dash record, or tear into him as you will.

In other words, act according to your comfort level.

Keep in mind, of course, that a threat is a threat to your body—not your ego. If you turn every challenge to your ego into an a socially violent situation, you'll probably get yourself arrested, if not killed. No, we're talking here about an implied or actual threat of physical harm. If it's less than that, you shouldn't be using violence; if it's more, you'll know it's time to use violence. This is the gray area you have to work out for yourself. This threshold point will vary from person to person based on life experience. Some people can stomach all kinds of crazy antisocial behavior; others will brook no threat whatsoever. Either way, it's a personal judgment call. This means your response to that stuff is up to you to figure out, for yourself, on your own time. We'll hand you the tool—you have to decide when you'll swing it.

Another reason people want all the upfront stuff is because they are not in a hurry to get to the wreckage. They're afraid. They want to stay in the semi-social realm for as long as possible and want to hang onto the idea that they are the Good Guy. If we maintain an attacker/defender dichotomy, e.g., 'he came after me, so therefore he's the Bad Guy, which automatically dubs me the Hero,' we keep things nice and social. And for us sane humans, social equals comfortable.

Remember, we have, as a species, a natural disinclination to violence; society wouldn't function if it were otherwise. Violence turns our stomachs. People will go to great lengths to avoid discomfort.

Do you really want to spend your precious training time working within your comfort zone in contrived, antisocial scenarios with only a small percentage given over to the actual work of violence?

Or do you want to work where actual change occurs, the point where all violent acts become the same—the point of injury?

Look at it this way: I could waste your time by having you role-play stage productions of Serpico such that for every 20 minutes of floor time you only get two where you're actually booting people. Instead, I'd have you experiencing violence for the full 20 minutes. Yes, half of that time is spent reacting for your partner, but you are still working where the buzzsaw hits the bone, at the point of injury. If you know what you're doing you can actually learn more about violence while reacting than when it's your turn. Ask anyone who's been used by an instructor for a demo. It's a difference you can feel (sometimes unfortunately so).

Generic, open, 'anything goes' mat time is the only 'scenario' you want to train in. To maximize your skill you need to practice that skill. In this case the skill is injuring people; it stands to reason that you want to spend as much time as possible at the point of injury. That's what mat time is. It's you, changing everything in your favor, taking control of the man, the situation, through injury. What came before is immaterial—it has no bearing on what you're doing to him. Did he yell? Or pull a gun? Did he grab you and knock you down? His ruptured testicles don't care. Neither should you.

Now, for all that, the single caveat: if your job is hallmarked by common occurrences that lead to violence (as in law enforcement or the military) then working those specific scenarios has merit. Car stops gone wrong, room searches that turn up enemies pretending to be friendlies; these scenarios are useful exercises for those who can expect to encounter them—but they're pointless for the rest of us.

Here's what it comes down to: use mat time to wrap and entwine the hard knot of skill within you, learn to use your mind as a weapon and your body as a tool for violence. Then you can walk the Earth free of 'rehearsal anxiety,' free in the knowledge that if your current problem—no matter how it developed or came upon you—can only be solved by shutting down a human being, you know where the off-switch is. And once you reach for that switch, all violent conflict becomes the same.

# Chapter Nine

## Kill The Unknown

*"The oldest and strongest emotion of mankind is fear, and the oldest and strongest kind of fear is fear of the unknown."*
—H. P. Lovecraft

Fear is a biological fact. We are hard-wired for fight or flight—remember, we're the descendants of the ones who didn't stop and think when the lion was bearing down on them. We're the kin of the ones who literally 'went ape' and flipped out with either a rooster-tail of dust to the horizon or by picking up a stick and getting busy. But just because fear is a biological fact doesn't mean that we have to give into it; we don't have to feed the fear, allow it to grow fat on the shadows of our nightmares. We can recognize (and be grateful for) the ass-saving properties of biological fear without bloating it out into the grotesquerie of all-consuming emotional panic.

We do this by killing the unknown.

Most people have no idea what goes on in violence outside of agony, mayhem and death. It is a Great Unknown; a bottomless, black abyss wherein we are free to paint our own personal pictures of horror with unthinkable outcomes. When you replace that unknown with knowledge, with understanding, governing principles and expected outcomes you take away the power of the unknown, starve it back down to a manageable size. Fear of violence and the unthinking, blind panic that induces becomes simple biological fear. Flight means you get the hell out of there. Fight means you stomp and tear and wreak horror upon the other guy.

There are two ways to make sure you're filling in the blank spots on the violence map, changing 'here be dragons' to 'boot to the groin.' The first (and most important) is asocial mat time;

the other is simple visualization. Both of these are the same thing: taking what is currently unfamiliar, frightening territory and making it understandable.

Each session of asocial mat time is an expedition into that Dark Continent, to lay bare its secrets, to find out that, indeed, there is no such thing as a one-eyed ogre with three arms that hungers for human flesh. Every single turn of asocial mat time is you answering the question 'what the hell goes on in here?' Turn by turn you answer that question, completely and with certitude: I crush his groin, I tear out his eye, I break his neck. That's what goes on in here. Mystery solved.

If you've trained at all you've probably had the 'zombie' dream—the one where you're tearing into this guy, breaking his leg, stomping his throat and he keeps getting back up. So you do it again. You do more. And still he rises and comes at you... Along these same lines we've all seen people that gave us pause, for one reason or another—he wasn't just big, he was enormous; he had a swastika tattooed on his face and looked like he was at the end of his rope made out of a last straw; or, without knowing why, he was just... scary. This is you remembering the tales of those one-eyed ogres that used to keep you up at night, and you're wondering if maybe there was something to the myth, and that something's right here in front of you.

You know he's human. He bleeds. And if he bleeds, you can kill him. You just have to remind yourself of this fact by taking a moment, whether right then and there or later (I recommend later so you don't set anyone off through body language), and imagine yourself breaking that person. One injury after another, putting him down and then ruining a perfectly good pair of shoes on him. Until he's a twist of flesh in the middle of a stain. Imagine it in slo-mo, one broken thing at a time, or speed it up, watch your favorite parts over and over. This is you, replacing a lie with two truths: you know how to do violence, and no one is immune. This is you, taking the time to remind yourself that there is no such thing as one-eyed ogres.

When violence is thoroughly mapped-out, option after option experienced in real-time on a real person, you know what to expect. There is no more 'unknown' to swallow you up in blind panic. As we replace that unknown with knowledge, we starve fear down to its biologic roots and inhibit its ability to grow unchecked through your mind. Instead of giving in to it, feeding it, helping it, you'll use it for what it's for—and put your boot in the other guy's groin. And after that the rest is academic.

# PART FOUR:


## THE LEGACY OF
## VIOLENCE
## - PEACE OF MIND

# Chapter One

## An Ounce of Prevention

*"If you could kick the person in the pants responsible for most of your trouble, you wouldn't sit for a month."* —Theodore Roosevelt

Traveling gives you a real perspective on how others view the United States, and it's interesting to see how U.S. citizens conduct themselves in a foreign land.

We've all heard of the 'Ugly American' syndrome, but I've noticed the 'Ignorant American' as being more prevalent. I've often said that we in the U.S. live in a 'Fantasy Island' situation when it comes to violence. Even though the world views us as a very violent nation we ourselves have the illusion that staying in our neighborhoods gives us a safety zone that allows us to be rude to each other.

By assuming we are dealing with others who fear getting sued as much as we do, some people in the U.S. are emboldened to push their verbal and nonverbal aggression to the max with little fear of facing a physical beating.

It's interesting how this U.S. approach can backfire when we project our imaginary legal safety-net over other societies where the rules differ:

A friend recently told me of a caustic uncle who traveled to Corsica for a vacation. He checked into his hotel and strolled over to the scenic marketplace to buy some fruits and nuts for his stay. His 30-year-old daughter (who was living there) was with him and warned him to not cross the street until the traffic light was green.

He ignored her and promptly stepped onto the street and was nearly run over by a nicely dressed man in an Audi A6. The uncle ran up to the car that was now stopped at the light and started screaming at the man with expletives flying. He then kicked the passenger door and waved at him with 'one finger' (this 'uncle,' by the way, is a 62 year old, distinguished looking attorney from Connecticut).

The response from the driver? He calmly got out of his car, walked up to the now emboldened uncle (who continued to spew invectives as the man approached) and without warning hauled off and smashed the uncle above his upper lip with a hammer fist (pinky side of the fist), instantly flooring the uncle and popping out five of his upper teeth. The man then calmly walked back to his Audi and drove away. All of this occurred in front of a large crowd.

The police took the report but chastised the now toothless old man, saying that in Corsica, they don't speak to each other that way unless they expect to fight. His daughter knew that no effort would be made to find the man in the Audi.

The uncle probably had responded to slights in his safe little enclave in Connecticut like that numerous times throughout his cantankerous life. Maybe his new dental work will be a reminder to be more civil. He was lucky he just lost some teeth.

This story occurred to me while sitting at the Madrid Airport at a cafe across from two U.S. soldiers. How do I know they were U.S. soldiers? No, they weren't in uniform, nor were they dressed like Americans. If it weren't for the fact that they both were sitting in broad daylight looking at their Army Service records, no one else would have known they were U.S. servicemen either. But every passerby took notice of the manila folders these two soldiers were poring over aimlessly.

I had to bite my tongue not to chastise these young kids. You'd think with the bombings and threats in Madrid over the past year they'd be a bit more security conscious. They could easily blend in with their civilian dress. But they just don't think anything could ever happen to them. It's always the other poor sap.

These are just two examples of people needlessly exposing themselves to potential violence. In one incident, violence occurred.

The other—so far, so good. When traveling it's a good deal easier to see lapses in judgment regarding personal security.

Ask yourself what risks have you taken in the last thirty days in your little world. Leave your doors unlocked? Take a risky short cut? Use an ATM after dark? Think a bit on that one.

Protecting Yourself and Avoiding Unnecessary Risks

Remember way back at the beginning of this book, we discussed how knowledge of violence tells you when not to use it? The goal of really understanding violence is a move away from social posturing. We've stressed again and again that you should never use violence unless you're in a life-or-death situation. That holds true.

So take steps not to put yourself in life-or-death situations.

Living in the United States, we really do have a mentality of "that could never happen to me." We hear about violence going on all over, but unless it's right next door—unless it directly affects us or someone we love—we continue to believe we're sheltered and somehow protected from criminal violence.

While it's true that we're fortunate not to live in a war-torn zone or a military police state, we have to acknowledge that there are criminal sociopaths running around out there, ready and willing to use serious force to get whatever they happen to want.

With that in mind, there are a few simple steps you can take to prevent violent encounters in your life:

- Lock your doors, including your car doors.
- Don't flash money around. Avoid standing by an ATM counting your cash.
- Don't allow someone who is clearly unstable to draw you into a violent encounter. Remember, it costs you nothing to walk away. You don't lose face by preventing a situation that can only result in serious injury or death to someone.

- Avoid dark, isolated spaces, bars known for trouble, or anywhere else you get an uneasy feeling. And encourage your family to do the same.

- Don't leave spare keys under doormats or in other ridiculously obvious places.

- Remain vigilant: keep your eyes open for dangerous situations and, whenever possible, avoid them.

As you can see, all of this comes down to a single statement: USE COMMON SENSE. You don't learn violence so you can walk around posturing like an idiot, you learn it so you know how to protect yourself when worst comes to worst. And if you can avoid worst coming to worst, well ... so much the better.

# Chapter Two

## Taking Control of Your Life

*"What man's mind can create, man's character can control."*
*—Thomas Alva Edison*

I was watching an Instructor Class one night with one of my great friends from the combat sports world and we discussed how difficult it is to talk about fighting to most people.

This difficultly lies in the fact that my definition of fighting is very different from what most people understand when they think of "fighters." When someone tells me they know how to fight, that triggers in my mind numerous examples of specific methods of inflicting trauma on the human body with the goal being the destruction of other guy.

In the rare instance when I decide to speak about fighting in a social situation, I usually regret doing so. Quickly I see that most people are uncomfortable with my very calm descriptions of the effective use of violence.

Most people get caught up in the surreal aspects of violence that permeate society today ... the sport or video game fake violence ... as opposed to learning how to methodically deliver systematic strikes to vulnerable parts of the human body with the goal being the total destruction of the other guy.

People always comment on how friendly and approachable I am—as well as my instructors. They are confused, I'd guess, because most of the martial arts and combat sport world is dominated by aloof personalities who seem more concerned with your recognizing their rank than having your questions answered.

I tell clients all the time that the more trained you are to deal with real violence, the more emotionally relaxed you become ... and the more you get to enjoy life experiences and people.

There's much less need to use false aggression in your demeanor to give off that 'FEAR ME' message. That's a fear-based protection mechanism, an act born of insecurity, that's mildly effective but ends up being exhausting to maintain.

This is yet another reason to seek out competent training in the use of violence. By facing the fact violence exists and learning how to effectively use it, you truly free yourself from unnecessary fear in your day-to-day living.

## Stupid Is As Stupid Does

If a killer kills someone, no one is much surprised. Likewise, if the killer is killed by his intended victim, it's just 'job well done.' But if no one meant to kill anyone, and someone ends up dead, well, then it's cartoon exclamation points all around. Everyone, including the newly-minted killer, is surprised. Cries of "How could this happen?" and "But I didn't want to kill him!" ring out. In the end it gets labeled as an unfortunate accident.

But these 'accidents' happen often enough that when a new one pops up I can still recall the last one I read about. Primates have a territorial dispute, and begin vocalizing at each other to communicate their displeasure, then aggression in a sideways request that the other capitulate. When neither one backs down, it goes to blows, again to run the interloper off. Usually, this works out fine, as nature intended. But when it's bodyweight + brain + concrete, one can end up running their rival not just off their territory, but off this mortal coil entire.

These things happen often enough that I would suspect you're more likely, on balance, to be involved in this sort of situation than purely asocial violence. In other words, you're much more likely to get slapped at than outright murdered. Misery comes from confusing the two.

If you train to kill and think that means you're physically trained to handle the antisocial, it's the same as carrying a gun in case you get into an argument.

If you train to kill and think that means you get to ignore the antisocial, you're setting yourself up to be ready for the most unlikely event while ignoring the most likely. Chances are, you're going to get caught wanting.

Because we train to use our bodies to cause injury, it's easy for people to get the wrong idea—on the surface, martial arts and combat sports look similar to what we do. And since martial arts and combat sports do a great job of preparing folks to navigate that antisocial fog-zone, then they tend to think we're training for the same thing, only in a 'super effective' way. That's like pulling a gun in a bar fight and 'shooting to subdue.' There's no such thing.

Still, people get all eager to lock horns. It's funny to me (funny strange, not funny ha-ha) seeing as how we can still end up with unintended fatalities. If you ask a gun owner, "How many gunfights do you want to be in?" the sane ones will all tell you, "None." The sane ones understand what goes on in a gunfight, and would never choose to be there if they didn't have to. If they should find themselves there, they will shoot to kill. But they don't walk around looking for gunfights.

Again, this is painfully obvious when we talk about guns. But for some reason it's less obvious with the empty hands. Why? It comes down to expectations. We expect someone to die if a gun is involved—that's what the modern handgun is for, killing people at close range. We don't expect someone to die from a standard, everyday session of monkey politics. And yet death is one of the possible outcomes.

Me, I expect someone to die every time violence is used, and then breathe a sigh of relief when everyone survives. I have absolutely no interest in going physical with monkey politics. I don't leave the house looking for opportunities to use my skills.

My aversion to violence runs so strong that it makes me something of a walking contradiction to my friends—I will do whatever I can to avoid physical, antisocial confrontation and yet won't hesitate to stomp someone into the morgue in the asocial realm. I'm like Gandhi with a nuclear weapon.

For those of you feeling eager, or emboldened by your training, some advice:

You're all set for the asocial. If someone wants to murder you, you're well prepared—knowledgeable, practiced, resolute. But don't forget to make sure you're prepared for the antisocial—sharpen those social skills, actively think about how you want to be in those situations. Will you join in and play along? Throw fuel on the fire? Push until he either backs down or goes for you? Or will you go completely sideways on him, defusing the situation, seeking to reduce his fear and channel his anger elsewhere?

Know where your triggers are and puts lots of padding between them and the outside world. Work to recognize when you're being pushed into a corner. And remember that simply walking away could save your life—or keep you out of prison.

As with the asocial, so with the antisocial: be prepared.

Chances are you'll go your entire life without anyone trying to kill you. I wouldn't make the same bet about some jerk calling you out.

**A Final Word on Antisocial Violence**

Whether it's a drunken barfly demanding you pay for an overturned drink or a posturing businessman, learn to recognize antisocial violence and don't let it control you. It's true that antisocial situations can become violent—but most of the time, they don't.

Learn to walk away.

Remember that you are in control. You know how to cause serious injury and death, which means you have the responsibility not to do so until no choice remains. Ironically enough, that actually gives you far more control over your life than you've ever had before.

Once you have the ability to:

- recognize and distinguish between social and asocial violence
- respond with deadly precision to a real violent attack, and
- control any situation so that you walk away with your life,

you become the one in charge.

This is the best thing about learning how to use violence, and the most compelling reason I can think of to recommend it, to have the ultimate control over your own life. Initially to preserve it, and then, once it's yours, to simply live it as you will.

# Chapter Three

## Treat Everyone Like They Are Six Seconds Away from a Killing Spree ... and Other Philosophies of Good Neighborliness

As you probably know by now, I hold philosophy and violence as separate entities. So while I used the P-word in the title, I am not saying that those who know or practice violence should subscribe to a single (or obvious) philosophy—I'm not saying "This is the Philosophy of those who know violence." Rather, I'm musing out loud on some of the choices I've made (and general trends I've noticed) in the way knowledge of violence changes the way people interact. With that out of the way, let's talk killing sprees.

As far as I'm concerned, the most important question that arises out of violence is: does knowing how to use the tool of violence inform your relationship with your fellow human beings?

There are really two angles to come at this question from: knowing what violence entails (or 'means') and knowing how to get it done.

In terms of knowing what violence entails, i.e., the terror and ugly finality of it, the trend is clear: intimate knowledge leads directly to avoidance. The more one knows about violence, the less eager one is to get involved in it.

Resolved, yes—eager, no.

This has a great deal to do with the narrowness of the tool; the fact that violence only does one thing—it shuts off a human being. The vast majority of your daily social interactions do not require this. It is unnecessary, therefore, to push social interactions in directions that could result in violence.

It also has something to do with the fact that really understanding violence removes the glamour. Once you've seen what the outcome of real violence looks like, you're not eager to play around with it. While four-year-old might think it's great fun to light matches and throw them away, an adult who's seen what fire can do will be infinitely more cautious and respectful.

Personally, I found I'm much more likely to capitulate and disengage by leaving the area, without a word, when confronted by someone with an obvious chip on their shoulder who has chosen me as the knock-off guy. Everybody wins—I sleep well and he doesn't get a broken leg just because he was having a bad day.

My brother, 'T,' tells a 'hilarious' story in which a man accosted him by saying "Let's fight!" and punching him (ineffectually) in the head. T thought about what that would mean—he saw himself breaking the guy's leg and stomping a mud hole in him on the ground and thought to himself, 'He can't want that.' So he said no. The guy persisted, again asking for a fight and punching T. (Again, to no effect.) Finally, my brother had it and shrugged, thinking 'I guess that's what he wants' and proceeded to make the guy's head and feet trade places with a single strike. It wasn't so much a 'fight' like the guy was asking for as it was a 'single man-stopping injury.' T knew that's where it would go (and more importantly, that it could go either way); knowing how serious it was made him uninterested in going there recreationally—if he didn't have to, he didn't want to.

I find that I am possessed of a saint-like patience these days—somehow, somewhere, I developed the habit of giving pretty much everyone the benefit of the doubt. I do not begrudge those who are curt and prickly their public anger and annoyance. I just figure there are extenuating circumstances I'm not aware of and I have no desire to be the next point on the down-trending curve of their bad day. I do my best to treat everyone with patience and respect—and how is that different, really, from treating everyone as if they were six seconds away from a killing spree? I'd much rather be the control rod in the nuclear reactor than the ignition charge in their personal H-Bomb.

This gets us to the second angle—beyond mere knowledge of violence and into confidence in how to get it done.

Nietzsche said that courtesy comes from a position of power. I would say it comes from both the knowledge of, and confidence in, violence. Politeness flows from a desire to avoid violence coupled with the knowledge that if worse comes to worst, the skill is literally in the palm of your hand. Socially, you have nothing to lose. People who seem impolite are really masking fear: fear that courtesy is a sign of weakness, that something is taken from them when they wait their turn or let someone else go first.

Knowing how to get it done removes the uncertainty from the extreme end of the scale—the answer to 'but what if he goes off?' is 'I'll break his leg and stomp a mud hole in him.'

And so I find myself in a the position of being resolved, but not eager. If I don't have to, I don't want to. If I have to, I will.

Our detractors would have you believe that we train sociopaths that our graduates are trained murderers ready and willing to kill at the drop of a hat. In fact, the opposite is true. The more you know about violence, the less you want to get involved with it. And the more you trust your own abilities, the less you have to prove.

It's not the strong and secure picking on the weak. It's the weak picking on anyone they think they can use to make themselves feel a little bit bigger. Once you understand violence and you're comfortable with your own abilities, everything like that seems to just fall away.

# Chapter Four

## Living a More Peaceful Life

*"I think that people want peace so much that one of these days government had better get out of their way and let them have it." —Dwight David Eisenhower*

In the end, the goal of all this training and hard work is not to run around in a hypervigilant state looking for trouble, waiting, taut with menace, for that guy's eye to twitch wrong so you can skin that smoke wagon and light the death-circuit or whatever.

The goal is to get to a place where you can forget you know this stuff.

How many times a day do you remember that you know how to swim? Unless you're a lifeguard, probably not at all. If you had to swim for your life, you would, and effortlessly so. But death by drowning does not enter nor haunt your thoughts. In fact, you may not have thought of it in a very long time, so long that the idea of it seems slightly silly. Especially where you are now, reading this in something resembling comfort and leisure.

That's what knowing how to swim does for you—one less thing to worry about. Let's not forget, though, that this one less thing you rarely worry about kills stadiums full of people every year. And you get to not even think about it. That's a Very Good Thing.

I'm here to tell you that the brilliant thing about knowing how to kill a man with your bare hands is that you only ever think about it when it comes up—whether you're in the middle of it (an occurrence about as rare as almost drowning) or when you're training for it (which can be seen as a 'recreational' use of the skill, akin to playing Marco Polo in the pool with the kids). The rest of the time, it doesn't even occur to me. I get to relax completely, even in public. When I'm not working, I can go weeks at a time 'forgetting' my expertise and what it makes me. But it's always there, silent and waiting, for the proper context to rear it's ugly head and bring it to the forefront. "Oh, that's right—gun means broken leg and throat-stomp."

But the rest of the time I'm not worried in the least. The perfection of the skill brings me peace. Ultimately, that's why I'm here, doing this work—so you can have some of that in your life, too.

It's ironic to think that learning violence brings about peace. It's the age-old paradox: if you want peace, you must prepare for war. If you don't understand violence, if it's a terrifying unknown that's only available to the criminal, you'll find it in places it doesn't really exist. Worst of all, you'll be stuck behaving like prey.

Understanding violence, and knowing when and how to use it as a tool, makes you walk like a predator. This is not the swagger and menace of acting like a tough guy; unconsciously you'll relax, breathe easier, and simply go about your business. Part of this comes from recognizing those loud, furious primate displays as just that— monkey politics. The rest comes from knowing that if things do veer into the black hole of asocial violence, it's your black hole, you've mapped the territory and a part of you lives there.

Just as predators can smell prey, they can smell another predator as well. When you walk around like you know what you're doing, paying attention but unconcerned, those hunting for easy prey will pass you by. You may save yourself from a violent situation without ever even knowing it.

And, given the choice, isn't that the best way possible?

## Living Without Fear

The constant violence around the world gets me thinking about how we respond to the idea of violence in general. One of the great things about really understanding violence is the fact that you get to live a more peaceful life. You realize you can only control your response to such events, not the events themselves.

Because you understand how to use the tool of violence, others who use it no longer threaten you. You realize what they are trying to do and that understanding goes a long way to deflating the intended effect: *uncontrolled fear*.

This doesn't mean these events don't have the potential for great violence but it does mean for the rest of us (who aren't the immediate targets of these acts of terror) that we may choose our response.

Some choose to alter their lives in hopes of avoiding violence. While prudent in some obvious situations (dark alleys, using bank ATMs at night, etc.) in other areas of your life such as traveling to do business and enjoying the world in general it gives those using the violence an unearned victory.

That's why I'm such a big proponent of learning how to use the tool of violence. In the military and law enforcement units I've trained they've seen reduced instances of excessive violence in non-life threatening events and increased effectiveness in putting down asocial violence.

I find the results even more dramatic for my civilian clients. It is a great first step towards reclaiming your life from unnecessary fear.

I strongly encourage you and those you love to start today and learn to take back your life from those who want you to live a life of fear. Seek out training in how to use the tool of violence.

There are many martial arts and combat sport instructors who do an excellent job showing their particular art. Some of what they teach is useful in the world of violence.

If you want the most direct path to using the tool of violence, then it's time to start applying the principles you've learned in this book. This is exactly what it's designed to deliver. Be smart about violence, educate yourself, and make it back home alive.

Madmen and criminals will be with us always; their heinous machinations will forever taint the symphony of civilization with a background hum of fear and dread. While it can't be ignored, tuning into it, giving into it, allowing that disharmony to dictate how you live and breathe grants them an unearned victory.

Don't dance to their noise. Take back that unjust, unearned victory.

After all, the second-worst thing you can do to them is have a great day.

# Afterword

## THE TFT DIFFERENCE

Training people to survive—and win—in violent conflict is deadly serious business. We understand that if we're wrong, people die. This base assumption is the foundation for everything we do. Not everyone feels this way, however—there is a wide variety of training choices in the self-defense world, some better than others. With all the advertising noise they generate it can be hard to figure out which is which—who has your interests at heart and who doesn't; who can truly give you the skills to prevail and who could be endangering your life.

To help you make an informed decision, you need to know the things that TFT does differently, what sets us apart from our competition and why. For starters, TFT is a team effort with nothing to prove. Your success is our sole motivation, and to that end we do our best to give you principles you can use, based on the observable facts of violence. We listen to you and use your feedback to improve our methods. This relationship benefits both of us equally—if we get better at training you, you get more of what you need to survive—and win.

### A Team, Not a Guru

A single person can have some good ideas, but without editorial oversight, or, more bluntly, 'no-men,' that one person's vision will tend to the myopic. They'll see what they like to see, what's easy for them, personally, to do. Without other points of view to provide critical challenge, that one guy is stuck with himself.

Where things really go to hell is when the cult of personality forms around him and he starts to believe his own press. Now he's not just stuck with himself, but on himself. His point of view is set in stone, and anyone learning from him is really just learning what works for the guru. He may be able to pull it off because of his unique set of physical attributes and skills, but the question is, can you?

If you can't, and he can't show you how without changing your physical attributes to match his (if only you were taller, faster, stronger), then what's the point? He may be able to survive violent conflict, but if he can't show you a clear path to that goal then you end up being nothing more than a faceless number in his ego-stroking throng. And that's not the reason you got involved in the first place.

He may be brilliant and charismatic and impressively skilled but if he can't swallow his ego and work to make you better than he is (or, at least, better than he was at your level) then he's taking your money, wasting your time and, worst of all, endangering your life. And all you get in return is the opportunity to bask in his brilliance and charm with the implied promise that maybe, just maybe, some of it will rub off on you. If you're lucky.

While not every guru is a charlatan, the above path is deeply grooved and well-trod in the self-defense 'industry.' We've watched good, caring people inadvertently fall into it and get stuck there. Even those starting out with the best intentions can end up enthroned atop a pyramid of well-meaning hero-worshippers. And that typically spells the end of any kind of meaningful innovation or evolution of thought, process and training. When this happens, the people on the bottom are the ones who lose out.

This is why Tim made a conscious decision not to be a guru. He founded the company, he leads the work and in that leadership role he is the recognizable face and eloquent speaker for that work. As an instructor he knew that his singular point of view and personal skill-set would not be enough to cover everyone because no one person, no matter how skilled, can. The seriousness of the work made that unacceptable. He reached out to like-minded experts and gathered a team of conscientious, highly-skilled instructors, some of whom were also physicians, scientists, writers, and thinkers. People who knew how to kill with their bare hands, and could communicate that skill to others. A pack of no-men to provide critical insight and peer review. A hundred years of experience instead of just a single point of view.

As a group, we are able to combine all of our skills and experience to make sure that you can survive—and win—in violent conflict, and make it back home alive. Regardless of your personal challenges, we can find a way to make sure you get the skill. And you can rest assured that you're not getting one person's take on what works best for them alone, but rather what will work best for you—when it really, truly matters.

**Nothing to Prove**

We already completed full careers of doing this professionally before Tim founded TFT. We literally achieved everything we thought we wanted to do with this stuff. Tim trained elite military groups all over the globe, federal agencies and law enforcement units, corporate security teams, as well as thousands of civilians. While I got a small taste of that, I really dove into the work of producing qualified instructors, ending up with 44 to date, seven of them Master Instructors with more than 10 years of experience each.

We had accomplished and experienced enough to fill a whole other book—a book of total awesomeness, if you ask either one of us. Of course, I'm being sarcastic. Maybe.

After almost 20 years, we both thought we were done. I know I sure was. I was in the process of hanging up my spurs and looking for that 'second act' in my American life. Tim was, as well.

But this work has a way of pulling you back in. It's a subject that almost everybody wants to know at least a little bit about. Many people were disappointed that Tim was calling it done; he began getting requests from individuals and groups to come out and do 'just one more' training. But 'just one more' lead to the next one, and before he knew it, he was pretty much full-time again. He pulled the rest of us in, one by one, and TFT was born.

So what does any of this, as 'impressive' as it may be, have anything to do with you? First off, it means we don't have anything to prove. We already got that out of our system. We're over all the chest-thumping, the posturing, the playing the tough guy with the chip on his shoulder. In fact, the whole reason we felt done in the first place is because we'd proved everything there was to prove. We trained people, they ran into deadly violence and made it back alive, whole—and victorious. Time and time again.

'Nothing to prove' means we can focus on you. You can be sure we're not out there to show off, or collect admirers, or find out if what we're doing really works. We don't have to be here—we want to be here. We want to be here for one reason, and one reason only: we want to give you the skills you need to prevail in the face of violence. Period.

The other thing you get is our experience. TFT is not a fly-by-night start-up that's experimenting on you. We're not freshly-minted black belts with a couple of years of teaching experience (which turns out to be the same year just repeated a couple of times). Tim and I have been doing this for more than 20 years each—every one of those a unique experience—it's never been the same twice. That rich vein of experience is what we mine to bring you the principles and methods you need to save your own life.

We have nothing to prove, and the only reason we're still here is because of you.

## We Actually Care

We view training you for violent conflict as seriously as teaching someone how to swim. On the surface the two might not appear to be related—violence is far more dire than goofing around in a swimming pool, after all. The common thread is this: if the instructor fails to impart the skill, the client could die. In swimming, the end result is a client who thinks they know how to swim while they really can't—a false confidence that can end in drowning. In violence, the result is a client who thinks they know how to hurt people, but really doesn't—a false confidence that can lead to their own murder.

This basic assumption informs and drives everything we do in TFT. In fact, it's the reason we do it at all. We're not in it for the money, or the ego-stroke, or to be international superstar badasses—we're in it for you, to make sure you have the skills to make it back home alive. When we train a group of 30 we don't see it as a single, anonymous mass; we see 30 individuals who each need to get it done right, and right now. We know we'll only have so much time with you—we have to assume we'll never see you again, that you'll have to rely on what we do at that moment for the rest of your life. We make that time count for you.

When I'm instructing I have to look you in the eye and know I'm not lying. I have to be sure that no matter how much time I get to train you, you walk out that door knowing how to injure a man, drop him, and make him stay there. Otherwise I literally can't sleep at night.

At the TFT San Diego Center, we thought it would be a good idea to let people come in for a free, hour-long orientation session. The initial concept was to get to meet each other, client and instructor, and to allow people to see what it was we were up to, learn a little bit about us, and experience a little bit of TFT physically. All to ensure that anyone signing up for on-going training knew exactly what they were getting into—and that it was exactly what they wanted.

It was just supposed to be a taste, not a full-blown training. It was the free sample to help you decide whether or not to buy the whole cake. People were not expected to be able to do anything at the end other than make an informed decision on whether or not to sign up.

That's not how it worked out.

Standing there, looking into their eyes, giving them 'just a taste'—enough to get into trouble but not enough to get back out again—felt terribly wrong. So wrong that the sessions turned into a one hour emergency crash course in TFT. The goal shifted off of a free sample and found it's way back to our core, founding principle: **make sure the client can get it done well enough to survive and win**. Can one hour make a difference? Well, it'll be dirty, and ugly, but if they do everything we told and showed them how to do in that hour, then, yes, it can.

We wouldn't sleep well if it didn't.

## Principles You Can Use

As instructors, what we can do in violent conflict—our own personal skills and abilities—means absolutely nothing to you. The fact that we know how to dislocate someone's shoulder and break their neck—after throwing them through the air—doesn't make you any safer. We're not your bodyguards, we won't be there when it's time for you to act. You'll be on your own, and it will come down to what you, personally, can do.

Showing you a fancy technique that relies on physical conditioning, coordination and years of practice is showing off. It may be impressive, and it may make the person showing it feel good, but it's not getting you any closer to surviving what could be the last day of your life. Looks great, feels good and it's of absolutely no use to you.

At a three-day seminar in Dallas, one of our instructors showed an awesome throw involving a shoulder dislocation. It was quick, dirty and got the job done in a single motion—tearing the shoulder out of the socket and dumping the guy on his head in one, easy step. Or so he thought. Everyone present was duly impressed and eager to get on the mats and try it ... and when they did, not a single person could get it done. Now, that doesn't mean some of them weren't close, but no one was doing it well enough for a life-or-death situation. In other words, some of them might have been able to pull it off—but not good enough to bet their life on.

In most training environments, the instructor would just tell you to keep working on it. This isn't necessarily a bad idea—as long as you have plenty of training opportunities ahead of you. These people had less than a day left. Six hours, and they'd be back on the streets, back into the rest of their lives. And they needed to be able to preserve those lives with what they could reliably do, right now. The instructor immediately scrapped the frustrating exercise and replaced it with a simpler, more direct and achievable way to tear out a shoulder and dump the guy on his head. While there were some who were disappointed that they weren't doing the 'fancy' technique, everyone could get the job done well enough to absolutely wreck the other guy. The instructor had ensured that when they walked out that door, everyone there could cripple a man and put him down such that he couldn't get back up. They could bet their life on what they could do.

Understanding why a shoulder comes out of the socket and how to make that happen are far more important than the thousands of different movements you could use to tear it out.

Instead of useless techniques, we give you principles you can use. Instead of an empty set of motions to mimic, we break out the principles that make those motions useful—the principle reasons why that motion causes an effect, how it achieves the goal of violence and gets you the injury you need. We get to the root, underlying rules that govern all violence and make sure you can get it done.

**Facts, Not Opinions**

There are an awful lot of different opinions out there regarding what to do when faced with the realities of violence. Unfortunately, a lot of those opinions aren't grounded in reality—they fly in the face of common sense, basic physics and physiology, and hard-won personal experience. Everyone is entitled to their own opinion, and that opinion may reflect their own experience and what works for them. It's when they attempt to extrapolate that opinion outward, beyond themselves, and impose it over inconvenient physical realities that they run into trouble. And if that's the guy you're learning from, it can mean trouble for you.

Reality is awfully inconvenient. It has a way of steamrolling right over flights of fancy—something that seemed like an incredible idea at the time, logical and enthusiastic-nod-inducing ends up flattened with all the best parts squirting out like a ruptured tube of toothpaste. It may have been a great idea, but the actual execution just doesn't hold up.

When this happens in training for violence, you're left with a choice: you can ignore reality and pretend it works, or you can swallow your ego and change what you're doing. This isn't an easy thing to do. There were lots of times when we wished it wasn't so. When a training method or a really, really cool technique turns out to be useless when compared against the physical realities of violence, it's a sad day. There are a lot of fun things we liked to do and train that ended up being just plain wrong, like practicing elaborate knife defenses. Working with the knife that way makes you feel really good—as you would expect 'not getting stabbed' to do—but it doesn't jibe with video evidence of stabbings. Or police reports from victims. Most people report never seeing the knife, or even knowing they were being stabbed. They thought they were being punched. It wasn't until they saw the blood that they realized something else was going on. This makes it highly unlikely that you'd even know you needed to do a knife defense technique, let alone execute it.

That inconvenient reality brings up another issue: if you finally realize (after being stabbed repeatedly) that a knife is involved, is going for a knife defense technique going to make a difference at this point? Or is it just going to get you stabbed more?

Realities like this challenged our assumptions and forced us to make the choice: opinion, or the facts? We chose the facts. The fact of the matter is you have to do what makes the stabber successful—cause injury. That's the only thing that's going to see you through. As cool as the knife defenses were to practice, and as comforting the idea of not getting stabbed is, none of that holds up outside of practice.

This is the process we used to winnow out the approaches that actually work from those that are just nice ideas, but wrong. We checked everything against videos of actual violence, police and coroners' reports, sports trauma medicine, and most importantly, the experiences of people who have prevailed in life-or-death situations. If it didn't match up, we chucked it, no matter how much we didn't want to.

In the end, we're left with a system that is internally and externally consistent, based on facts that you can check for yourself. Don't take our word for it—opinions have a way of going in and out of favor, but the facts remain the same. If you're going to bet your life on anything, it should be the facts.

## We Listen and Adapt

Most importantly, we listen to our clients: what they find useful, and what they don't. What they want and need, and what they don't want to be bothered with. At every training seminar we hand out questionnaires to find out how the participants felt about the experience; we take their responses to heart and change our training methods accordingly.

The most notable example of this was when a client noted that a small, informal session highlighting a number of different ways to access the eyes—different angles, body positions and with several different tools—made a huge amount of sense. It was what allowed them to finally 'get it' in a way that the preceding 'technique-based' part of the seminar had not. This forced us to confront the issue of whether to train people the way we had learned it, or to train them the way we understood the material now.

This one comment from a client changed our entire training approach—we literally tore it apart and reassembled it from the ground up. Instead of training techniques with a specific set of movements (and then hoping the clients could pull them apart to find the base elements), we trained targets exclusively, showing them how to crush a throat standing, from the side, from behind, with the man on all fours, and laying down, then with the client on the floor, etc. The results amazed everyone, instructors and clients alike—what once took three days to instill we could now do in one day. And then, with a little more effort, half a day. Returning clients, those who had trained with us before the methodology shift, were astounded at how good the new people were in such a short time.

To this day we pay close attention to what our clients have to say about their experience and progress—we never know when someone will point out the next big improvement in our methods.

Our goal is to give you the best training possible—you're the reason we're here and your success is all we're really interested in. TFT is the perfect intersection of the actual facts of violence presented by people who know the subject cold and really just want you to get it right. That's what motivates us—knowing that after you walk out that door you're a little bit smarter, a little bit harder, and a lotta bit better at using the tool of violence. Your success is your survival, and having you make it back home alive is why we're here.

# To Learn More About Target-Focus Training

To learn more about how Target-Focus Training enables you to defeat anyone threatening you or a loved one in an unavoidable violent confrontation, please see our website at http://www.targetfocustraining.com or email us at:

**tft@targetfocustraining.com.**

And be sure to sign up for Mr. Larkin's highly regarded FREE newsletter, "Secrets For Staying Alive When Rules Don't Apply."

You'll also find DVDs and other Target-Focus Training materials at:

**www.targetfocustraining.com/products_training.html**

Each year a limited number of live training events are scheduled. Here you learn the complete Target-Focus Training system, in 16 hours—guaranteed!

To see availability or reserve your spot in one these unique live sessions go to:

**www.targetfocustraining.com/live_events.html**

or email us at:

**tft@targetfocustraining.com**

For other product questions, contact us at

The TFT Group
c/o Straitview Publishing
325 E Washington St, #207
Sequim, WA 98382

206-686-3469

To learn how to apply the physical
tools of violence you've just finished
reading about in this book,
we're gifting you with...

# 30-Days of FREE Access

to the ultimate,
online training experience!

To begin, simply go to:

**http://www.targetfocustraining.com/tftmonthly**

or call us at **206-686-3469**
for more information.